Mindful Relationships

Build Nurturing, Meaningful Relationships

by Living in the Present Moment

Oli Doyle

Copyright © Oli Doyle 2017

The right of Oli Doyle to be identified as the author
of this work has been asserted in accordance with
the Copyright, Designs and Patents Act 1988.

This edition first published in Great Britain in 2017
by Orion
an imprint of the Orion Publishing Group Ltd
Carmelite House, 50 Victoria Embankment,
London, EC4Y 0DZ
An Hachette UK Company

1 3 5 7 9 10 8 6 4 2

All rights reserved. Apart from any use permitted under UK copyright law,
this publication may only be reproduced, stored or transmitted, in any form,
or by any means, with prior permission in writing of the publishers or,
in the case of reprographic production, in accordance with the terms
of licences issued by the Copyright Licensing Agency.

A CIP catalogue record for this book
is available from the British Library.

Paperback ISBN: 978 1 4091 6748 8

Printed and bound by CPI Group (UK), Ltd, Croydon, CR0 4YY

Every effort has been made to fulfil requirements with regard to
reproducing copyright material. The author and publisher will
be glad to rectify any omissions at the earliest opportunity.

www.orionbooks.co.uk

ENTRY

The Mindful Living series

Mindful Relationships

Withdrawn from Stock

3 8002 02320 567 9

Also by Oli Doyle

Mindfulness Plain & Simple
Mindfulness for Life
Mindful Parenting
Mindfulness at Work

To you, whoever you are, who seeks light
in the apparent darkness.

Coventry City Council COU	
3 8002 02320 567 9	
Askews & Holts	Jan-2017
158.2	£12.99

Acknowledgements

Gratitude beyond measure to my teachers along the path: Nirgun John, Ekai Korematsu Osho, Byron Katie and Eckhart Tolle, and to all who laid the foundation for them. I can never express my thanks.

Thanks eternally to Ren, Liam, Freya and Ezra, you're all just perfectly mad and I love it. Thanks to Mum and Dad, and to Phil and Abby for all that you do, and all that you have done. It means a lot.

A humble bow to my mindfulness family all over the world who keep in touch and share the journey with me. Thank you for walking this path together.

By day, I get to practise all this with Kate, Karen, Jaz, Kris, Anne, Gabby (Gabs), Sue and Lou, and I miss practising it with Danny and Jess. You guys are the best. Thank you forever.

It takes a village (almost) to write a book. Thanks to Jill and Sarah from Orion for all your help and support. None of this happens without you. Thanks to Jane from Graham Maw Christie, agent of the century and great value.

And finally, thanks to *you*, for being ready to change your world. I'm right here to help, whatever you need.

Contents

Introduction

Relationships are wonderful, aren't they? They bring joy, happiness and love into our lives . . . except when they don't. And when they don't? Oh wow, they are absolute hell, aren't they? Pain, sorrow, sadness, grief . . . It's a horror show!

In the midst of all that horror (or all that joy, for that matter), it *appears* as if the other person is the cause of it all. If only they would . . . or if only they would stop . . . then I could be . . . You know how it goes. But what if the whole thing was happening in you, and what if you had total control (and total responsibility) over whether it was joyful or horrible? What if nobody else needed to play along?

Imagine if you could be happy and peaceful now and always. Imagine if you already *were* at peace and experiencing happiness now, but you didn't know it! Well, that is how it is.

For many years I chased along the well-worn path of seeking happiness through approval, love, acceptance and all that stuff. It was exhausting and unstable, with highs when everything worked out and crashes into the depths when they didn't. And eventually I realised that it was all in my head. The whole thing was made up of stories, of thoughts saying, 'You did well. They all love you,' or, 'That was terrible. Everybody hates you.' It was *that* voice that controlled the ups and downs.

So gradually, I began to wonder, what if no one else needed to do anything different for me to be happy? And I began to investigate.

When I looked deep within, I discovered that I was at peace all along, happy and content. I was just a little confused about who 'I' am. I believed myself to be the mind, the thoughts, and I identified with what they said. And it was the unsatisfactory nature of the world (when viewed from that perspective) that pointed the way home. I'm so glad now about everything that didn't 'work out'.

The fact is, we have it all upside down and backwards. Relationships are not there to make us happy, and this is not a book on how to be 'mindful' in order that your relationships will work. In truth, relationships *are* mindfulness practice, and they can point us to the obvious fact that we are already complete, peaceful and content. We just don't notice because we are so lost in mind stuff.

The old way of living, as if others are in control of our happiness, is both disempowering and frustrating. It leads us to try to control the world around us, especially our loved ones, in the hope that, if they change in the right way and it sticks, or if we can find and keep the right one, the one for us, then this aching in our heart will dissolve.

As it turns out, though, the aching in your heart is only there because you are off seeking happiness outside yourself. Out of this belief that you are not enough, all sorts of madness arises, and as your attention moves out from your perfectly wonderful self to the world *out there*, a yearning arises, urging you to come back.

The mind sees this yearning as evidence that something in the world needs to change, that you don't have enough of something, and as it seeks, the body follows. And you know where all this leads.

This book is here to show you the way back to yourself, back to who you were prior to thinking, concepts and that image your mind has created of 'you'. Relationships are great fuel for this homeward journey because they are fickle, unpredictable, and often unsatisfactory to the mind.

But if you use the opportunities that your relationships bring to keep looking within, to keep finding out who you are underneath all those thoughts, then the journey is greatly rewarding. You will find yourself in love every moment, with yourself and your world, and what others do won't matter so much anymore.

How to read this book

This book is designed as a six-week course, and you can use it that way if you wish, reading a passage each day and doing that day's activity. Alternatively, you might like to choose a day at random, or read a few days at once. My only suggestion, though, is to make sure you take the time to try the activities, which is where the words become yours, so to speak. As you read, the words may make sense or not, but in the practice itself, you will be able to check what is real and true for you.

I am more than happy to support you on this journey, so feel free to email me at oli@peacethroughmindfulness.com.au, check out my closed group on Facebook – Mindfulness with Oli Doyle – or track me down some other way. I am on this journey too, as you will read, and I love to hear from fellow travellers.

So, without further ado, let's begin our journey together. Make sure you have supplies (a cup of tea will do) and that you are ready to dig up some old truths and look at them under the microscope. The road can be a bit bumpy, but you are as safe as can be right here, so let's start on this adventure of discovery and exploration.

This is the most rewarding trip you will ever take – the trip into yourself.

WEEK 1

Together This Instant

Relationships, as we think we know them, don't exist. That is a bold statement to start a book with, but there it is: what you think is happening isn't. And this week, we will explode some myths (pop!) about relationships, myths that keep you constricted, trapped and dependent on others for your happiness.

You see, almost every belief that we are taught as we grow up is limiting, unhelpful and a little bit crazy. But because everyone else believes the same thing, those beliefs seem quite legitimate. I won't try to replace those beliefs this week, but I will ask you to question them, based not on belief but on your direct experience. Here are a few of the beliefs we will examine:

1) Relationships exist primarily as shared experience over time.
2) I need good relationships with others in order to be happy.
3) What my loved ones do affects how I feel.
4) I have relationships with other people.

Now I know what you may be thinking. These do indeed seem to be universal truths, but as you will discover this week, there is more to your experience as a person than you may have realised. So let us begin with the belief that underlies all the others: the belief in the reality of time.

Day 1: Together This Instant

As I sit here and type, I am aware of movements in the rest of the house. My wife and three-week-old son, Ezra, are in the next room doing their night-time dance and I can hear the rustle of Liam and Freya, my six-year-old son and three-year-old daughter, in their bunks every now and then. My mind can tell the story of my relationship with each of them, especially my wife Ren, whom I have known for many years, so we have a lot of shared history, or so it seems.

But where is this history? What evidence is there that anything has ever occurred between us? In truth, it's all a story. Right now, there are no thoughts arising in my awareness, no stories, and therefore there is only this. There is no relationship with anyone. For a human to say this is strange, to say the least.

Human relationships are based almost entirely, it seems, on shared stories, on memories and plans. 'Remember the time we . . .?' and 'I can't wait until we . . .' are the two basic formulae, and all relationship stories are a variation or a combination of these two. To have a relationship, then, we need to roughly agree on our story of the past, we need to both believe that this story is positive (or positive enough, anyway). And because the past is the driver of each person's view of the relationship, we can spend more time analysing what happened and what it means than we do experiencing our time together.

'What did she mean by . . . ?'

'Why didn't he smile when I suggested that?'

'She doesn't like me, I'm sure of it.'

These stories are often stressful, because your thinking mind believes that you are not good enough, and that it is only a matter of time before everyone else realises that too. If you have ever watched every reaction, every facial expression of the person you seek to please, you will know what I mean. I lived like this for many years, monitoring the responses of others to what I said and did, and keeping mental score of who liked me and who didn't. It was exhausting.

Today, that seems a distant memory, but I remember what it was like. When I meet people now, I actually meet them *now.* I'm not planning our future together or analysing our past, I'm enjoying being with them this very instant.

And so it is with my family too. Of course I remember their names and birthdays, but the primary focus of my time with them is what is happening now. And when they aren't around, I focus primarily on who I am within that instant.

This is the essence of a life of mindful relationships: you only ever relate to those you are with now, and when they are not around, you leave them alone mentally. I still organised a Mother's Day present for this weekend and started getting Liam's birthday present ready, as memory and planning is fine when it comes to practical matters. But the heavy, fearful, angry and stressful stories about what did or didn't happen and what I need (or what I need to avoid) in order to be happy simply do not arise, or at least I don't believe them.

Activity – When?

Close your eyes and think of someone who is important in your life. In your relationship with that person, is the main focus your present moments together, or the past and the future? Take a moment to consider this.

Feel the breath in your lungs, become alert and aware, and picture yourself interacting with this person as if there were no past, no future. Imagine what that relationship could be like if the fear and the desire that come along with those thoughts could not pollute the connection you share.

Ask yourself where your shared past exists. Beyond a thought in your head, what evidence do you have that this story is true? And what about the future you hope to have with this person. Where does it reside? Is it a real thing, a solid experience, or a thought, a projection?

Sit with these questions and allow the past and the future to reveal themselves for what they are: helpful concepts that we can use to organise our lives, not the holders of truth, nor of salvation.

These are the roles we assign to our time-based stories. The past is the truth, it's what happened and I know what it meant. The future is what I need to complete me, to be happy. Both these roles are false.

Time will not bring fulfilment, as it doesn't exist. Your whole life happens now, and the thoughts we call time (memories and projections) are merely tools we can use to plan and learn. In relationships, our focus on time can deaden our experience with others. Actually, 'time' can be substituted here for 'thinking';

they are the same thing. And if you are busy thinking while you are with another person, you miss *really* being with them.

If, on the other hand, you are mindful when you are with them, if you look, listen and breathe with awareness, then you will find your experience together coming alive.

Day 2: I Don't Need Your Approval Now

The second belief that rules most relationships is that we need approval in order to be happy. Many people (myself included) have grown up feeling that they were somehow not 'good enough' and have learnt to seek approval from outside as a way to cover up that feeling. The satisfaction that is derived from this type of approval is very shaky indeed, as it hinges upon the continuing participation of other people, who are generally more concerned with their own lives than with our need for their validation.

This approval-seeking puts everyone in an uncomfortable position. It puts unreasonable responsibility on the other person, whom you rely upon to give you a steady stream of recognition. It also puts you in the awkward and difficult position of trying to figure out what the other person wants and doing what is needed to please them, even if it contradicts what is right for you. All of this manipulation can lead to resentment when the other person doesn't live up to their end of the bargain, when you bend over backwards and it still isn't 'good enough'.

And the curious thing about approval is that it is tied up in the thinking mind's desire for the perfect future, the 'happily ever after'. The mind believes that once enough approval is acquired, the feeling of unease that lies within will disappear, and you will finally be happy. And when will this event occur (hopefully)? In the future, of course!

And so, we can end up in a real pickle, doing things now that we hope will lead to approval and recognition in the future, and constantly evaluating the responses of others to see if we are on the right path. How exhausting!

But what about this very instant? Do you need approval now? What if that imagined future dissolved and you only lived to enjoy this moment? Would you still feel the need to chase approval from your loved ones?

What you will discover, if you go deeply into your actual experience, is that approval-seeking relies on time and on thinking in order to survive. To chase that recognition in the first place, you have to examine the past, make a plan that will lead to being accepted in the future and then keep analysing what happens to measure your progress. These are all thought-based activities, so if you live in the now, they dissolve.

If you are with someone without thinking, just there as awareness, there is no possibility of getting lost in this process. You will simply enjoy being with them in the moment, without worrying about what they may think of you, or whether they might stay with you or leave you in the future.

And when you connect with other people in this way, two strange and counterintuitive things happen. Firstly, there is a deep sense of peace and contentment. Actually, this feeling is natural when you are not seeking anything outside of what is now. And secondly, people tend to like being around you. After all, who wouldn't want to spend time with a calm, peaceful person who listens well and can accommodate any point of view? That sounds like a good time!

And although it may sound as if you need some complicated and gruelling training in order to relate to others from this Zen-like state, the truth is (thankfully) much simpler. All you need to do is replace your seeking with a little curiosity.

Activity – I Don't Need Your Approval But . . .

Close your eyes and bring to mind a recent interaction in which you were desperate for the other person to think well of you. This might have been at work or at home, but take a moment to find a situation in which you were checking the other person's responses, thinking about what to say next and hoping that the future outcome would be favourable.

Remember how you acted and how you felt in that situation. What did you say and do to try to curry their favour?

Open your eyes and shake out the tension of that situation, breathe with awareness and smile at your mind's antics for a moment.

Perhaps we could sum up your guiding belief in that situation as 'I need your approval' and we have seen where that led. Next, I invite you to replay the situation, but with a different philosophy in mind. Say to yourself, 'I don't need your approval but I'm fascinated to see what happens next.'

Close your eyes and revisit that scenario, but this time bring curiosity about what the other person was saying and doing. Imagine that you were watching a riveting movie, completely absorbed in what was going on, enjoying every moment and watching with alertness and clarity. Take a few minutes to relive what happened with this new approach, and to notice once again how you would have felt and behaved with this different attitude in your heart. What difference does a little curiosity make?

If I don't need your approval now, I am free to do my absolute best in every situation without worrying about what will happen next.

Play with this shift this week and see what happens when you put down the search for approval in your relationships. You will be amazed how freeing this small change can be.

Day 3: Knowing What You *Really* Need

In relationships, especially those that are intimate, a widely held social belief hides and causes all sorts of problems. We believe that we need others to love us and to show that they care, in order for us to be happy. Each of us has different requirements around this, a different story about what 'love' looks like, and when your partner doesn't meet that so-called need, conflict is often the result.

If your partner is quiet and reserved, and you want them to talk, ask questions and look into your eyes when they speak, you will be disappointed. If you want your partner to give you some space when you get home from work, to leave you to yourself at certain times (and to guess when those times might be), and they are intense, extroverted and energetic, you will be disappointed. And when that disappointment arises, your mind will blame the other person.

In truth, these beliefs and expectations create a gap, because they are unrealistic, they do not match up with life as it actually happens. The mind then tells you that life is the one that should change. 'I know what's best,' says the mind, 'and that's not it!' He should speak in *this* tone, with *that* look in his eyes, not like that!

This gap happens everywhere in our lives and, until we start to notice what is happening, the mind sees life as the one with the problem. In this case, life is represented by your partner, who is clearly getting in the way of your happiness. The mind says, 'If only he would do such and such, then I could feel happy again.' This approach is hopeless.

To believe you need another to change in order for you to find happiness is a trap. It puts you at the mercy of the other, and it makes them responsible for your inner state, which is insane. Who else could be responsible for my inner state but me? If I am the one who feels angry, or sad, or disappointed, that feeling is arising in me, so why would I ask someone else to manage it for me? 'Please don't do that because I don't want to deal with that feeling,' says the mind.

This is equivalent to my son Liam's insistence that it is his sister's fault that he pushed her, because she didn't move when he asked her to. I understand this reasoning in a six-year-old, but I feel a bit embarrassed when I notice this pattern arising in me.

My wife Ren and I have very different styles of being. Where I want to talk and explain and question, she wants to get the job done. Many times I assumed that this meant she didn't care, that she wasn't interested, and I moped around with that 'nobody loves me' face. I thought, believed, in that moment, that if only *she* would change to be more like my image of how she should be, then I would be happy.

In fact, if she had changed, I would have found something else to be unhappy about, because unhappiness is the underlying state of the human mind. Seeking is the movement of the mind and dissatisfaction is both the cause and the effect of that seeking. When you look for something outside of now to bring happiness, you move out of alignment with life and it feels uncomfortable. This discomfort justifies more seeking because it seems as if there was something missing from this moment.

What you need, what we all need, is not a life of perfection (according to your mind). What you need is to live in alignment with the present moment. This is why life doesn't give you what you want, but instead forces you to look within yourself to find that happiness. For this reason, nothing and no one can ever really fulfil you.

Activity – What I *Really* Need

All your life you have probably believed that what you needed to be happy was something that would come from outside of you. Today, for 24 hours, try something different: act as if you needed yourself instead.

Close your eyes and take attention deep into your body. Notice your breath coming and going, and sense the peace that is there underneath the turmoil of thinking and emotions.

Say to yourself, 'What I need is to be here now' and stay present and alert. Stay with this practice for a few minutes.

This week, whenever you believe you need someone else to change, close your eyes, say, 'What I need is to be here now' and breathe mindfully. Watch what happens when you take the responsibility away from others, and grab hold of it yourself instead.

It turns out that your partner can't make you happy or unhappy. They do certain things, you tell a story about those happenings and then you make yourself happy or unhappy. When this was unconscious, you had no alternative, so don't regret the past hurts you could have avoided. Celebrate the fact that now, in this moment, you have a choice. You can continue to blame others for your unhappiness and to suffer. Or, you can come back to what you really need, to what you want deep down.

And if you take this path, you will discover that everything you wanted is what you already are. Nothing else is needed but a simple shift from seeking joy in the things that happen to noticing the joy that is in you already when you return continually to your life in this instant.

Day 4: Only One Relationship

Although it seems, from a conventional point of view, that we have many relationships with many different people, the experience of life is a little different. Your mind may not like to acknowledge it, but in reality, your only relationship is with yourself. Everyone else comes and goes.

Think about it. Who do you spend your entire life with, every single second? Who is there when you wake up and when you drift off to sleep at night? It's all you.

Now I am not denying the existence of other people, nor making some philosophical argument about the nature of the world, I'm just saying that you are the only consistent person in your life.

Of course, it doesn't *seem* like this. It seems as if your best friend is there with you too, sharing your life, but she isn't. It feels that way because the stories we tell about other people seem to keep them alive in our minds, even when they are somewhere else. The person who is with us is actually a collection of memories, of thoughts, not a real person at all.

If you watch closely, you will discover that, in fact, there are only three types of people in your life. One type is yourself, the eternal friend (or enemy) you spend your whole life with. The second type is the person you are with right now, the one you appear to be relating to. And the third is the imagined people, the ones constructed in your mind.

Anyone who is not with you now exists only in thought, as a memory or a future projection. And whoever is with you now is a part of your present moment experience.

While this may seem confusing at first, it actually makes life incredibly simple, as those three types of people are all easy to take care of. Firstly, you can take care of yourself by following your breath, being aware of your body and staying mindful, which makes every moment a pleasant one. You can take care of those who are with you now by staying mindful, listening to them, paying attention and doing the best you can in the moment. And those who aren't with you? You can forget about them, unless you want to send them a birthday card or give them a call. Otherwise, they don't exist.

In 'normal' human life, the opposite is true. People put more energy into thinking about the people who aren't with them now, remembering the past and planning the future, than they put into being with the people who are here now. And it is rare for most humans to acknowledge their inner experience, let alone have that awareness as a key part of each moment.

A friend dropped in yesterday and while she stayed, she was the only person in the world, apart from myself. We chatted, laughed, drank tea, and then she left. All of a sudden, she was gone, and the only evidence I had of her existence in this world was a thought, so I left her alone. I didn't spend a second wondering what she thinks of me, whether she likes me or what advice I might give her. Instead, I moved on to the next thing. My son and daughter came into view and they were the whole world, along with my inner experience. And so life continues.

Activity – Starting With You

It is possible to stay connected with your own inner experience, even while you relate to other people. I call this 'Starting With Me', and I find it a wonderful way to stay anchored in the present moment and tuned into myself while I spend time with another person.

This practice is simpler than it sounds. To start with, just notice your breath as you move through the world and relate to other people. Feel the breath and live your normal life.

As this becomes comfortable, go deeper into your body in situations that don't require too much thinking. For example, when your partner or friend is telling you a story, feel your whole body as you listen. This won't detract from your ability to pay attention to what is being said; in fact, it will enhance it. Stay alert as you listen and be there totally, without needing to analyse what is being said.

In any interaction, you can either get lost in thought or stay present, and these tools can help you to become more mindful in your relationships with others. Try them today and see how your experience of life begins to deepen.

When you try it, you will find that starting with you, making your experience primary, strangely makes you more available to help other people. This is because being mindful allows us to directly experience the encounter, instead of thinking about it (or thinking about something else).

The usual way of relating is scattered, distracted and, ultimately, self-centred, because it is focused on what the other's words and actions mean to you. Start with you, however, and you will be available, present and alert, prepared to be there for the other in whatever way they need you in the moment. What a wonderful way to live.

Day 5: No Time, No Conflict

In any relationship that lasts long enough and is deep enough, it is likely that you and the other will, at times, disagree. These disagreements can be simple or complex, rare or common, low-key or intense, and this will determine, in many ways, the quality of the relationship.

If you often have complex, intense disagreements, for example, the relationship will be turbulent, which some people love and others hate. A relationship with rare, simple, low-key disagreements, however, will be pretty quiet and relaxed.

But these descriptions only apply to relationships that are ruled by the mind and by thinking, also known as 'normal' relationships. The norm for humans is to have regular bouts of frustration, of resentment and perhaps of arguments, as each mind tries to get its so-called needs met by getting the other person to do and say certain things.

Conflicts happen in roughly this order:

1) Someone does something.
2) The mind analyses it and argues with it.
3) The mind creates a story about what happened and makes an identity for the other person (for example: she's rude, he doesn't care about me).
4) The mind projects into the future and tries to plan. What will I do to stop this? How can I prevent it from happening again?
5) We return to Step 1!

From Step 2 onwards, you will feel stress. By the time that stress arises, Step 1 is in the past, and all the other steps happen only in your head.

It seems as if these disagreements arise because the other person is not playing their role properly, not doing as they should. But if you look closely at what happens inside you, it will become clear that underneath every seeming conflict sits the belief in time.

Think about it. When you get upset with others, is it about what they are doing in this instant, or is it a memory of some event from the past? Is it because they are causing you a problem now, or because they are doing something that may get in the way of your future plans? Take a genuine look inside and see.

A few weeks back, my friend Andrew was telling me about some relationship conflicts he had with some family members. As he described the 'problem', it was interesting to notice when all these things took place. Andrew spent half the time talking about 'What they did', and the other half describing

'What they might do' and 'What I need to do about it'. Past, future, past, future. This happened, that might happen, this might happen, that happened. And so the mind rolls on.

Conflict doesn't always mean open disagreements with others; in fact, mostly it only happens inside. And what we are in conflict with, primarily, is our story of the past. Often, the other person has no idea that there is even a problem.

And so, conflictual situations can play an important role in our lives, as they bring our habitual focus on time into sharp relief. This is the first step towards dissolving it.

Activity – The Beginning of Time

Imagine that your way of living consists of two modes: 'Now' and 'Time'. These modes are very different: one is the experience of life as it happens, the other happens through thinking about what happened and what might happen.

And imagine that there is a little gauge inside you showing which mode is active now, which one you are living in. Stress tells you that you are in Time; peace tells you that you are in the Now.

Close your eyes and think back to a recent conflict situation. It might be one that led to discussions and arguments, or it might be something that no one else knows about, a conflict that happened purely in you.

Take a few minutes to go back through what happened and see if you can pinpoint the beginning of Time, the instant in which your mode of living changed.

Watch the event and try to isolate the moment the stressful stories took over from your actual experience. Take your time and be gentle with yourself.

Continue this as a regular practice whenever you feel stressed and you will find something interesting: problems never happen now, they're always rooted in past and future.

Bring this understanding into your day-to-day life and you will start to *feel* Time taking over in real time, which opens up a choice about whether you continue to indulge those stories or whether you snap back into Now.

This choice then becomes available to you always, all because others didn't do what your mind said they 'should'. How wonderful!

Day 6: True Connection

In intimate relationships especially, we seek to connect with others on a deep level. We seek this, and we can be scared of it at the same time. More accurately, your mind is scared of it, and with good reason.

Your mind wants something from the other person. It has created a story of the perfect future and cast that person in a role in it. This 'perfect future' might be the rest of your life, or it might be the story of a pleasant Sunday afternoon. It doesn't really matter.

In the conventional sense, the depth of the connection you have with the other is based on the seeming importance of that story in relation to your future hopes and the amount of time you have spent together. If that person is 'your wife', then a large amount of your future story may involve her, and your mind may have invested a large amount of energy in thinking about and evaluating the relationship already.

This person, then, is also a threat to that future, because they might not do as they should! They might leave, or change, or not show up. They might die or get sick, or they might not want to be a part of your story anymore. Relationships, and people, are more fragile than we like to think, and they all dissolve eventually, so the mind is constantly in a fearful state because the future is uncertain.

Is this true connection? Thinking about what you want someone to do and then feeling pleased when they do it, and upset when they don't, doesn't seem particularly connected. It seems a bit selfish. And is it a connection if most of it happens in your mind, through thinking? Can you connect with someone outside of the now?

In my experience, it is only possible to connect with the person you are with this instant, and everything else is a story. After all, how can you connect with someone unless you are interacting in this moment? There might be energetic ways of connecting from a distance that I don't understand, but for most of us, connection means being together now in some way. This might be through the phone, the internet, or even in the moment of writing someone a letter, but it is not through thought, not in your head.

The mindful way is simple. Connect in the instant of togetherness, then forget about it and be present with what is. When my family wakes up this morning, I am there as fully as I can manage. Right now, they're asleep, and so they aren't a part of my experience, there's just me.

And the connection you form when you are here now is much deeper, more intense than when it is based in thought and in time. This type of connection requires you to be alert and present, as you need to let thinking stop in order to connect.

Normal relationships unfold like a soap opera, in which you need to remember the last episode to keep up with the story.

In mindfulness, there is no need to remember anything except the practicalities (where your friend lives, your partner's name, etc.). There is no need to construct a mental image of that person based on what they did last week and therefore what type of person they are. Just be with them now and then leave them alone.

There is an old Zen story of two monks walking in silence, who come to a muddy stream. A rich woman is at the stream, abusing her attendants for not being able to carry her across (because they are carrying all her stuff). The older monk bows, picks up the woman and carries her across the stream, then keeps moving. They walk on. Several miles down the road, the younger monk says: 'Why did you pick up that woman back there? She was rude and ungrateful.' The older monk smiles and says: 'Dear friend, I put the woman down hours ago. Why are you still carrying her?'

This story raises an interesting question: are your relationships happening in the present moment, or are you carrying a bunch of images around in your head?

Activity – Put Them Down

Close your eyes and breathe. Feel the air flowing in and out and leave your mind alone for a moment.

For a few minutes be with yourself only. Take attention to your inner experience and notice what thoughts, feelings and sensations are arising now. Don't get lost in them, though, just watch.

Carry on with your day, and see if you can do the following:

- Be completely present in your interactions with others (or as much as you can manage).
- Notice how your mind wants to carry images of those people around, long after they have left.

See if you can keep returning to what is happening now, even though your mind wants to drag you back into the past.

Relationships are actually simple. You sit or stand, talk or listen, stay or go. But the stories the mind wraps around these simple relationships are incredibly complex, making it seem as if relationships (and life in general) are complex too.

Don't believe your mind, or me. Try this way of relating as an experiment and see what happens in your life, and allow your relationships to come and go in this instant, the only one there is.

Day 7: The Space in Relationships

Stress, it seems, is normal in this human world, as everyone rushes this way and that, seeking something they don't yet have. Relationships become another field in which this happens, as people seek this or that through interactions at work, at home and out in the world. And after all this seeking and rushing about, many fall into bed exhausted, not by what they did physically, but by the mental gymnastics that go on all day. By all that seeking.

But there is a wonderful, healing space available within your relationships, one that is simple to find (once you start looking) and one that can transform your experience into one that is calm, peaceful and quiet. The space of silence.

Most of the time, we are thinking. We're weighing it up, trying to figure it out and wondering what the next step should be. And so, when you are with someone else, it is quite possible that you are primarily thinking about what they are saying and doing, what it means for you and what you should do or say next. This happens because we have a future hope that we're aiming for, so this moment is merely a step along the way.

Look at your actual experience, though, and you will discover that the present moment is all there is. Nothing ever occurred outside of it, nor can anything do so in the future. Your whole life is just this, just now.

And if you leave the future and the past alone for a moment, and just be with someone, you will discover that, in most relationships, you don't need to do or say much. Your mind *wants* to say a lot, but it is not necessary in many cases. In these moments, you can instead rest in the space of listening, without needing to do anything.

For example, when your partner, or someone close to you, has had a hard day at work (or a hard week, month or year), and they are telling you all about it, the mind will get a certain urge. The urge is to tell them how to fix it or to get on-board with the story and join in talking about how terrible it is and how it shouldn't be so. This leads to advice (which hardly anyone wants) or getting lost in the story with them, which is usually not helpful either. And both of these movements feed your mind and bring you deeper into the thrall of thinking.

There is another way, however, and it is simple, powerful and enjoyable. It is called just being.

Activity – Just Being

The next time someone is telling you about a hard time in their life, try doing this instead.

As your friend or loved one talks, listen carefully to what they are saying, but don't respond unless it's absolutely necessary. As you listen intently, notice the gaps in what they are saying, the silent spaces between words and phrases. Listen to that silence with as much intensity as you listen to the words.

For that moment, don't think yourself into some role as a friend or confidant, just be there as a listener, just be. Allow the other the space to explain, the space to be heard, and trust that they know what to do next, or they will when they need to.

You might say some words or make some sounds in order that they know you are listening, and that is fine. But keep it brief, open and don't go into the story. For example, you might say, 'It sounds like you're having a tough time,' or you might reflect back what the person said. But beware! Your mind will want to become consumed in the juicy details of the story, the gossip and intrigue. This tendency is baked into humanity and those stories can draw awareness in just as your mind's stories do.

You can go back to the old way, getting lost in the story, any time, so on this occasion, try staying free and see what it is like.

This practice of being the space, being the listener, just being, can draw you out of the habitual tendency to get lost in story. And when you can listen to another without getting lost there, it is far easier to listen to your mind without getting lost there!

And, as an added bonus, playing this role in the lives of our loved ones can provide a space for healing that isn't possible when we're busy lamenting, planning and strategising. At first, others may be uncomfortable with this approach to relating, or they might be hoping you will stoke the fires of drama as you did in the past.

But, over time, as this way becomes your way of being, others will start to embrace and enjoy it too, or they will find someone else to throw fuel on their stories, and that's fine too. The question is, do you want to stay lost in these soap operas, or do you want to be at peace?

WEEK 2

Curious Partnership

Curiosity is an energy that enlivens and refreshes relationships, moment after moment, and in many relationships it seems to evaporate over time. When you know a person well on the level of the mind, a feeling of staleness can creep into the relationship, as there is nothing more to 'know' about the other. Then, many relationships survive through a shared sense of past (reliving old experiences) and future (planning the next thing).

But the most enjoyable relationships have a consistent spark to them, a sense of freshness whether it is the first meeting or the 500th. And if you look closely at those relationships, you may notice that there is a sense of spontaneity, of unpredictability to them. These relationships are grounded in the present moment, and our interaction now is what matters.

For most, these types of relationships are rare, but it is possible to relate like this in every interaction you have. And it is as simple as noticing with curiosity.

To be curious is to look, listen and experience with an open mind and heart, wondering what will happen next. It is to bring awareness to what you see and hear without judging or trying to control it. And it is to find wonder and simplicity in the miracle of being together, here and now.

This week we will explore two things: how to use the experience of being in relationships to discover and bring out your curiosity, and how to bring that curiosity into relationships more fully. Of course, the two complement each other.

While it may seem overly simplistic to the mind, if you experiment with curiosity in your relationships, you will discover that it can quickly transform them from stale and frustrating to enjoyable and fresh, without the other person needing to change one bit.

Day 1: Curious Play

In the beginning, many relationships have a joyful, playful quality about them. There is an energy of freshness and newness, and often because we don't yet know the person well, we are surprised and delighted by their actions.

Over time, though, we get to know the other person's mind, we get to know their conditioning, and we think we know them. And when this happens, everything becomes predictable and maybe even a little boring. Or does it?

Before we continue, though, let me be clear about what I mean by 'mind' and 'conditioning'. The other person's mind is their thoughts, beliefs and opinions about various things, as well as their likes and dislikes. Their conditioning consists of their predictable, conditioned response to various situations. So if your partner says she hates Christmas and then is grumpy every Christmas Eve, her mind and conditioning are working together to make life unpleasant.

Early on in relationships, many people try to keep their conditioning hidden, out of fear that it might send the other person running for the hills. Therefore it is often later, when we feel confident that the other person will stay around, or when we can no longer keep that conditioning down, that our seemingly true self emerges. Of course, it isn't your deepest self, it is your conditioning and mind.

As a result of this pattern, the grass can seem greener in new relationships that have not yet gone stale, and the mind can become dissatisfied with the familiar, especially in intimate relationships in which you might live together for many years. But is it possible to maintain a fresh energy, even when the relationship has been going for years?

Actually, something even better is possible: an ever deepening relationship that unfolds in the now, with the energy of curiosity at its core. And that is where we begin this week.

The seeming curiosity that arises in 'normal', mind-driven relationships is a little different from the energy of mindful curiosity. The mind is curious because it wants to feel safe, secure and protected by being able to predict what will happen in the future and plan accordingly. The curiosity that arises beyond the mind is pure wondering, a deep sense of awe and mystery that has nothing to do with the past or the future.

So while the mind catalogues and compares, awareness notices what is arising now and loves it wholeheartedly. And while the mind laments what has been lost from the past, feeling nostalgia and melancholy, awareness is only concerned with what arises now. Here's how it works.

Activity – Playing With Curiosity

Pick two relationships, a new one and an older one, and try this little experiment this week.

In the new relationship, instead of thinking, analysing and cataloguing the other person, look at them with intense presence, right here and now. Watch them and listen to them without seeking to understand, to get something from them, or to figure out what they are thinking. Respond to them instinctively, with spontaneity and joy.

In the older relationship, see if you can leave your beliefs about the other person alone for a few minutes and be with them mindfully. Watch, listen and respond out of awareness of this instant, and see how it feels to put down the burden of the past in your relationship for a moment.

In my own life, I have experienced these two ways of relating many times, and as I have moved more deeply into the present moment, relationships have become fresh, fun and interesting. Even with my wife Ren, who I have lived with for 13 years, there is a deeply joyful sense of curiosity. We laugh a lot, crack many jokes and play in this moment. Early on, when we were both lost in mind, there was novelty in the relationship, then it started to feel stale as we got to know each other and spent a lot of time together.

Looking at the cause of this staleness (my mind) helped to unpeel many layers of conditioning, many layers of mind, and this has left me free to be there as awareness in the relationship, not as a conditioned thought pattern.

Relationships, therefore, can help us to rediscover the energy of play and of curiosity, which are essential elements of our true nature. And as we practise relating with the energy of curiosity, all relationships become mindfulness practice. When this happens, it doesn't matter whether your mind likes the other person or not, you can be with them quite happily because no judgement arises and there is nothing you want them to do differently.

And finally you become someone who others enjoy being around, purely because you changed your approach, from mind-based knowing to aware, alert curiosity. This dissolves old conflicts, removes old relationship patterns and allows us to live each moment with clarity and compassion, all from a simple little change.

Day 2: What Do *You* Want?

Much of our relationship energy is tied up in the search for approval. We want others to think well of us, to love us and to show that they care in certain ways, which are different for each of us. This approval-seeking arises because we are out of alignment with ourselves, and we believe that someone outside of us will be our salvation.

But, in reality, the happiness that comes from a positive relationship is only a pale substitute for the joy that arises from reconnecting with your true self. If you feel the sun reflecting off a mirror, then step out into the warm sun directly, you will feel the difference in intensity. Seeking happiness from a relationship can only lead to temporary reflected happiness, like mirrored sunlight. To experience the full intensity, we must turn our focus 180 degrees and look within.

Today, therefore, we will explore how searching for your *own* approval, instead of the approval of your partner, friend or colleague, can fundamentally change your experience right here and now.

The unspoken inner question the mind wonders about as we seek the approval of others is something like, 'What do you want?' We try to figure out what those around us like and how they feel about certain things. And then we moderate our behaviour, change what we think, wear, do or say in the hope that someone else will say, 'You are good enough. Congratulations!' The mind almost imagines that there is some sort of championship, with medals handed out, and that we will be on the podium, will be the best, if only we can figure out the right way to be.

So, of course, most people feel like frauds, although few will admit it. If you spend your day moulding yourself for the benefit of others, it will feel less than genuine. And when others don't seem to approve (because they are too busy seeking it too), there can be a sense of frustration, of resentment, because the plan didn't work.

Activity – What Do *I* Want?

But the question, 'What do you want?' is a good one to ask, if you turn it around 180 degrees. Ask yourself, 'What do *I* want?'

Don't ask your mind, though, or you will be furnished with a list of desires, like my boy Liam's letters to Santa Claus, and these desires will live in the future and be outside of yourself. Instead, ask yourself what *you* want. Let the question rest in your open, clear awareness and see what arises.

To put it another way, this question doesn't begin as a wish list of outside things, but as simple curiosity. What do I want right now? How do I want to be in this moment? What resonates with my deepest self?

Also, this question doesn't need to be answered in words, in thoughts, as the question itself is the important thing, not the answer. The question redirects your attention within, and once you return attention to your inner world, the answers will come, will seem obvious, at the right time. The answers must be lived, and they must be lived now.

Take a few minutes to introduce this question into your awareness. Ask it in your mind and then sit and breathe mindfully. Don't expect any answer, just practise sitting with the question.

Then, when you have choices to make this week, use this same question when you feel unsure, then make the choice that feels right in the moment. This may feel disorienting at first, but stick with it, and see what happens.

As I sit and ask this question myself, the answer, if there is one, is a resounding, 'I don't know', but in each moment of my life I can feel what is right for me and what isn't. When I feel stressed or upset, I know I am out of alignment with life (although I might blame someone else temporarily!). What I want is to sit here and type, until that comes to an end, but deeper than that, I want to live in harmony with life as it is. I want to live as peace in this instant.

Liam has popped out to join me, so obviously life is telling me that writing time is almost over for today, and what I want is to go with that.

When it comes to relationships with others, it is easy to ignore your inner voice and go with what you think will make another happy. If your partner invites you to see an action movie and you couldn't think of anything worse, it might feel risky to say no. What if he gets upset? What if he doesn't want to be with me anymore? These and other questions arise unconsciously, driving our responses without us knowing.

But try introducing this new question consciously instead, and you will find yourself becoming slowly more in tune with your own heart. And don't worry, this won't lead to a life of selfish action, as what resonates with your deepest self is usually also what is best for those around you, even if they don't like it at the time.

Day 3: Relating Beyond Belief

Beliefs rule in human interactions. What you believe about a relationship, and about the other person, drives the way you behave towards them. And what they believe about you influences the way they act towards you.

And then, as things get really messy, what you believe they believe about you affects what you believe about them, and then you're in a real pickle!

Our minds genuinely believe that they can understand and know others, that it is possible to know what they think and who they are, but let's check that against our actual experience.

Can you ever know what someone else thinks? Can you ever know what their experience is like? Is it possible to truly know another person as you know yourself?

In the reality of my experience, everything I think about another person comes from my mind interpreting the things I see them do and hear them say. And even with those I spend the most time with, I witness only a fraction of that external behaviour.

On top of this, I have no clue about their inner world. When my wife says she is frustrated, I don't know if that means what it means when I say it. When my friend says she is happy, I have no idea if that's true. And, perhaps most importantly, I don't know what other people think of me, and I don't care much either!

Why do we spend so much time and energy trying to figure out something that is completely unknowable? Because the mind wants control. It wants to feel safe and comfortable, and the illusion of knowing gives us a little taste of this.

I say 'the illusion' because what the mind constructs is no more than opinion. It creates stories about other people, telling us who they are and, more importantly, who we are in relation to them.

In my own relationships, this belief structure has been dissolving for many years, since I started moving out of thinking and into awareness. I used to relate to my loved ones primarily through thought, and therefore my mind's judgements about them were the main way in which I decided what sort of person they were. At the same time, my assumptions about what they thought of me, especially whether they liked me or not, were influential in determining how I felt about myself.

So if other people didn't respond in a way that I believed meant that they thought of me as a good person, I would feel anxious, worried and fearful, and I would try to change to be more likeable. I spent years figuring out how to be as likeable as possible, and I got pretty good at it (I think). But it was exhausting and I felt like I was on a constant roller coaster, going up when someone laughed at my jokes and sliding down (or plummeting) when they didn't.

As I started to observe my thoughts more and believe them less, it became apparent that I have no clue what anyone else thinks or feels. It also stopped mattering whether they seemed to like me or not. Actually, that's not quite true. What has happened is that now I don't even notice whether they might like me or not, I don't analyse their behaviour for signs of approval. I'm just there with them.

When I talk with someone these days, I am interested and engaged, but I have no interest in trying to figure out their inner world. I am enjoying my inner world so much that I can leave theirs alone.

Activity – Beyond Belief

Today, when you have an interaction with someone you know well, try this. Before you meet, bring your attention intensely into your body, come into the present moment. When you meet, look at them with curiosity and stay alert and attentive to what is happening now.

Notice where your mind goes, what old thoughts, beliefs and emotions arise, and be curious with them too. They are part of your experience now. As each belief, thought or emotion arises, acknowledge it with your attention, but stay primarily focused on the interaction you are having with the other person. There is no need to change or get rid of that mind activity, but don't let it consume you.

As you relate to the person with more mindfulness and less mind, notice how it feels to spend time together in this way. How does this compare to the old, conditioned way of being together?

And as you become more confident in this way of relating, try it with people your mind doesn't like, or resents. This will bring many hidden beliefs to the surface, as well as deepening your mindfulness practice as you stay present even while your mind is screaming.

Mind, thoughts and beliefs have been the vehicle for human interaction for a long time. But as you start to awaken from that, you have a choice. You can decide to relate from this deadening realm, or you can embrace the freshness and freedom of present-moment relationships. Play with these two approaches this week, and you will quickly see which one feels more peaceful and authentic for you.

Day 4: Curious Communication

Relationships often start with curiosity, as you wonder where he is from, what she likes to do on the weekends or what he thinks about global warming. This is the exciting part of the relationship for many people, as there is a sense of freshness, of learning and of novelty about your interactions with that person.

As relationships progress, this curiosity can become dampened as the mind discovers all the story-based facts about the person, their past and their hoped-for future. And as this sense of wondering dwindles, it is replaced by the knowing of the mind. I know what that person is like (and I know what they *should* be like). I know what they need to do for my happiness. And I know where this relationship is heading (or at least where I want it to go).

All this knowing, of course, is imagined. How can you know anything, let alone everything? You can have some ideas, some opinions, some instincts, but how can you ever know anything outside of yourself completely?

As well as being mind-generated, this 'knowing' quite naturally reduces the sense of wonder and discovery in the relationship. This loss of wonder doesn't happen because relationships get stale over time, it happens because you stopped looking and listening. When you didn't know the other person well, you needed to look and listen carefully, your mind was invested in this because the unknown is mysterious, interesting and a little scary. The unknown might lead to our future happiness, or it might bring future disaster, so the mind is both drawn to it and fears it at the same time. This gives that initial curiosity a lot of energy.

There is, however, a deeper curiosity that arises from a state of mindfulness. We could even say that this curiosity is one with that state of mindfulness, it is one aspect of this way of being. This mindful curiosity is your natural state when you are not busy thinking, and that thinking is synonymous with the sense of knowing that deadens the wonder of relationships.

When you look and listen to another person without thinking, judging and analysing what they are saying, curiosity is natural. When the need to figure out what they are doing and what it means drops, there is an openness, a sense of wonder that is energising and fulfilling.

And when you infuse this way of being into relationships, something magical starts to happen: the relationship itself becomes curious, open and peaceful. And bringing that sense of wonder back is all in the details.

Activity – All in the Details

Close your eyes for a moment and use the awareness of your breath to bring your attention into this moment. Feel yourself breathing and allow your attention to move from thinking to experience.

Open your eyes and, in this state, look around. Look with open, curious interest and take in as much detail as you can. Notice the objects around you, their shape, colour and texture. Look at the space you are in and observe the boundaries you can see, be they walls, the horizon or something else. Be there totally, look with your eyes, not your mind, and be still.

As you do this, listen carefully to what you can hear right now. What sounds are arising? Again, listen without labelling, judging or analysing those sounds. Just listen.

Now think of someone you have known for some time, someone with whom you feel you have lost that sense of curiosity. This could be your parent, your child, your partner, or anyone you have known for a long time.

The next time you are with that person (this could be in

person or on the phone), watch (if you are with them) and listen with clear, focused awareness. Forget for a moment about what you need from them, what their words and behaviour mean or what you need to do next. When you need to know these things, they will be there. Instead, just be present with them now.

As you do this, notice as many tiny details as you can about that person. What are they wearing? How do they move? What is the intonation of their voice as they speak? Take it all in.

Feel free to speak, respond and interact, but allow these reactions to come out of that alertness, not out of the thinking mind.

What was it like to spend some time just noticing, just being with that person in a state of awareness? Did it change the energy of the relationship?

And what if every moment of your relationship had this mindful curiosity infused into it?

Doing this as a couple, or as friends, with both of you practising this awareness together, is twice as much fun, so try sharing this activity with a friend and trying it out the next time you are together.

Relationships don't get stale because of some inevitable decay, they get stale because we stop noticing. The novelty wears off for the mind and it looks for the next thing.

But if you bring this noticing practice into your relationships deliberately and without thinking, then every interaction becomes an adventure.

Day 5: Why Do You Feel That?

It might seem a bit odd, but it is possible to be curious even when you are upset, angry and frustrated, even when the relationship seems to be going wrong. Sometimes I wonder if this is what relationships are for!

Normally, we don't like relationships to push our buttons. We want others to work around our 'needs', massage our egos and generally keep us happy. We act as if our happiness is a balloon that needs to be protected from prickles lest it be popped, but this is not true happiness, it's a shallow type of satisfaction based on the world giving us what we want.

Real happiness is natural, unconditional and unshakeable. It comes from knowing who you are beyond thinking, and it has nothing to do with anyone else.

Interestingly, the prickly behaviour of the people around us can help us to discover this true happiness, if we know how to work with the feelings that arise when the balloon goes pop.

My relationship with my kids is great for this. Every day we bang heads, they do things that push my buttons and bring old conditioning to the surface. Bedtime is the best time for this. You see, around 8 p.m., my mind starts planning what needs to be done next and willing the children to go to sleep *now* so I can get on with it. Sometimes I laugh at this, and sometimes I get lost in it.

And when I get lost in it, like I did last night, something fascinating happens: a tightness arises below my ribs on the left side of my body. When this feeling comes, I remember to be curious, to ask myself, 'Why do I feel that?' and to sit with it. This is an old feeling, and it has nothing to do with my kids. It is triggered by my thoughts about what they are doing.

If they were more compliant at bedtime, I wouldn't get to find out about this hidden feeling, it wouldn't arise. But life, luckily, is great at making sure we are pushed to experience these old bits of conditioning, and they are brought to the surface to be experienced directly.

All that old conditioning needs is to be experienced, to be acknowledged and to be allowed to be. If you can do this, it moves, changes and is gone. If it stays hidden, on the other hand, it will keep driving your behaviour from below, without you ever quite knowing what is going on.

And so, those spiky people who know how to push your buttons are the best ones to spend time with. Relationships that challenge you are the best type for growth, and if you make this a deliberate practice, it can be even more powerful.

Activity – Out With the Old

When I have these prickly experiences in my relationships, my first attempt is usually to avoid them. I try to change the situation, to talk the person around or to run away, and then I remember that this is an opportunity.

After this remembering, I do the following, and you can use this to allow the past in you to be uncovered and experienced.

Sit still and take your attention into your body. Find the part of your body that is most tense, or where the strongest sensation is.

Once you discover that spot, focus all your attention on that sensation. Be totally present as you watch that feeling, experiencing it completely.

Don't go off into story. Stay with the actual feeling.

Don't try to change it. Go deeply into the feeling.

And allow that feeling to be there and to stay with you, for as long as it does. Just watch.

Try this practice whenever your old buttons are pushed this week and see what happens when you give these old feelings space to be processed.

When I say 'the past in you', I mean the old emotional energy that has not been experienced. When these emotions are avoided in some way, they are stored in your body as stress, anxiety, worry, anger or other difficult feelings.

The feelings themselves are not a problem. They are merely emotional energy. This energy is like water, and the usual way of dealing with it is similar to stuffing fallen leaves into the gutter. Eventually your house will flood!

Feel them directly and these blocks will clear, and you will then feel the flow of energy that is natural for all beings. Your loved ones cannot make you feel anything, but they will show you where the blocks are when they trigger those old feelings.

Normally, we blame our loved ones for the feelings, but this week, you can take responsibility for your inner state and in the process your loved ones can help you to find freedom from the past. How wonderful!

Of course, if your relationship is abusive or your safety is at risk, this is a different matter and I suggest you seek help to find safety. If you're in a safe relationship that pushes your buttons, though, take full advantage and be thankful. In this case, the bigger the challenge, the deeper the learning.

Day 6: Breaking Open

There is something about relationships that has the ability to break us wide open. Left alone and undisturbed, it is possible to wrap a protective shell around your beliefs and your ego, and you can (mostly) manage day-to-day life in such a way as to avoid the experiences that might crack that shell open. Of course, life brings difficulties and frustrations, but these tend to be more superficial, whereas the experience of a deep relationship brings a sense of vulnerability that we rarely experience elsewhere.

Breaking open like this can bring fear to the surface. We may have spent years cultivating that protective shell and having it taken apart can feel overwhelming. Today I will share with you a different approach to unlocking this shell gently and on purpose, using the opportunities that intimate relationships provide. This way is enjoyable and empowering, without the sharp ups and downs that happen when life smashes that protection for you.

If you look at it, the shield we cultivate is not so much armour as a way to hide things we don't want to look at. It is like a locked chest deep inside, in which we can shove all the unpleasant things we would rather not see, like that cupboard in the hallway that you dare not open in case the contents burst out and squash you!

For me, 15 years ago this chest was filled with two main ingredients: the belief that I wasn't good enough and the fear that others would find out. I discovered many ways to keep this chest locked, by keeping others at a distance, using humour to divert attention and by never looking in there myself. I perfected the art of being charming and fun, and

I would hide away when I didn't feel charming or fun, or I would pretend otherwise.

This was such a well-practised routine that I didn't even know it was a routine. I thought that was who I was!

And then, I moved in with my girlfriend. Oh dear. All of a sudden, there was someone asking, 'Are you OK?' when I wanted to hide. There was someone who saw through the pantomime and knew, on some level, that I was faking it. All of a sudden, I felt I had to look in that chest.

It's no coincidence that around that time I became interested in meditation and found my way to Zen and to mindfulness. The suffering that came up when that chest started to open was pretty intense, and it forced me to choose: run from the situation or start to look inside. I resisted for as long as I could, of course, but eventually I took the second option.

Perhaps you have had a similar experience, or are having one now. Or maybe you feel there is much that you have buried and you are worried about looking down there. Whatever the case, it is possible to make a smoother, gentler transition than I experienced, by bringing curiosity to your inner world.

Activity – Looking Within

That ego shell, it turns out, is wrapped around your self-image, not your self. It is there to protect something that doesn't really exist, except as a story in your mind. If you apply curiosity to this self-image, it can gently unravel, leaving you free to be yourself without all that fear.

The process is quite simple. Close your eyes and remember a time when you felt emotionally threatened in your relationship. This might have been when you were criticised by your partner, when you were fearful that someone would leave you or when some other situation left you feeling lost.

As you remember the experience, some of the emotion may arise too. Feel yourself breathing and ask yourself the question:

'Who was I protecting?'

Repeat the question in your mind without trying to answer it. Ask the question, then sit in the silent space that follows and allow your attention to be drawn deeper within. Who is the one you were trying to protect?

Don't get drawn into the mind's stories about that situation, instead go deeper. Who were you trying to protect? Does that someone actually exist? Can you find that self that felt threatened? Be curious.

Don't give some philosophical answer either. You need to experience the answers, not think them. Sit with curiosity, with not knowing, and allow your attention to be drawn ever deeper.

Connection brings the promise of future fulfilment, which is why mind-identified people (as I was) seek out relationships. On some level, we believe that this person will bring us lasting happiness.

But as that connection deepens, to the mind it brings the threat of annihilation. This person may discover that I am a fraud, that my whole self-image is a projection, and that I am not the person I am pretending to be. In some relationships, there is an unspoken agreement never to go there, never to challenge the other's self-image to the point of collapse, an approach that may lead to 'comfortable suffering', as I like to call it.

The other options are simple: run away or go inside and find out who you are underneath all the stories. As the truth of this reveals itself to you, the connection deepens further, more layers crack open, and you are left as a freer, happier human being.

Day 7: Not Knowing Why

As humans, we want to know what caused a problem. We want to explore the reasons behind what happens so that we can improve life, change it and make it easier. And while this approach works well when it comes to the outside world, to improving systems and to getting your car fixed, it creates many problems when used in relationships.

Imagine, for example, that your best friend is less reliable than you. You love her and she is great, but she tends to go missing, or not show up at times your mind says are crucial. And then a moment comes when you believe you need her, and she isn't there. It would be completely possible to spend hours, weeks, months, even years thinking about what happened and trying to diagnose the root cause. Why did she do that? What does it mean?

'I think it's because . . .'

'The way I see it, she just can't . . .'

The mind believes that understanding the past is the key to happiness in the future, because once all the problems of the past are remedied and the perfect future is constructed, all will be well. But the reality of this approach is that it saps your energy and your attention, taking it away from your actual life and putting it into the imaginary life in your mind.

I find it helpful when working with my mind to consider thinking or contemplation on two levels. Level one is practical thinking, in this case, 'She's not here. What will I do?' This is the calm, peaceful approach: '*What* will I do', not the hysterical: 'What will I *do*?'.

On this level, we are simply moving towards the best option we can find in the moment, free of anger, sadness or stress.

The next level is that analytical thinking with which we are all familiar. 'How could she leave me like this? She must think . . .' This thinking serves no purpose in your life, but to the mind it is wonderful. Have you noticed how much enjoyment your mind gets out of thinking about (and maybe talking about) other people's so-called faults? It improves our imagined self-image by tearing down our image of someone else, and it is a great distraction from the other thoughts, about what is wrong with me.

Thinking at this level is unnecessary. It doesn't move you towards a resolution and it takes precious attention away from your life. Often, in these situations, there is nothing practical you can do, because the situation has finished anyway, or you have no intention of doing anything about it. Why mentally pull it apart then? Because the mind loves it.

But what if you could let go of this level of thinking whenever it didn't serve you? What would it be like to live without this stressful activity? It is completely possible, and the way to do it is to get comfortable with not knowing why.

Activity – What?

The peaceful approach to dealing with relationships with others is to move your focus from figuring out why they did that to considering what you need to (or want to) do about it, if anything.

Take a moment to bring to mind a relationship situation – recent or old – that led you down this path of trying to figure out why someone did something, why they are the way they are, or what it all means. I remember spending hours of my life reliving encounters with others and trying to figure out whether they liked me or not, for example. Take some time now to remember your own example.

Close your eyes, feel your breath and ask yourself, 'Does that situation need my attention?' Or, if it is an old situation, you could ask, 'Did this situation need my attention?'

Take a few moments to breathe and wonder whether there was or is a need to put attention into that situation. If the answer is yes, see what ideas for actions arise out of the present moment. If the answer is no, just be here, breathe, and let the memory of that situation be there in your awareness for this moment.

When situations arise in your life now, you can use this same question to see whether practical action is needed or not. Your mind may continue working on understanding the problem, because that's what it likes to do! But if you see that such figuring out is unnecessary, you become free from it, and eventually your mind will stop.

Try it this week. See if you can reserve your attention and energy for those situations that require them now. And see if you can leave the mind to analyse and figure out, without getting lost in it. And if you find yourself lost in such thinking, notice that, and come back to this moment.

When we get comfortable with not knowing why people do things, we are left to focus on our responses. As you practise this, you may notice that many situations don't need any response at all, and in those that do, you will conserve your energy for the doing, rather than wasting it on circular thinking.

WEEK 3

Playing Together

Play is curiosity, and mindfulness, in action. It is the natural tendency of the universe to engage in it and it is ours as well. True play requires you to be fully engaged in the moment and to do so without thinking about the past and the future, beyond what is needed. And the energy that it brings is enlivening, joyful and healing.

In relationships, this playful energy is often there at the start, when everything seems new and shiny. But as time goes on, that energy can dissipate as we go back to our usual way of being: planning and remembering, planning and remembering.

This week, I invite you to use the relationships in your life to rediscover your inner playfulness, your inner sense of fun and mystery.

Day 1: Play For the Sake of It

When was the last time you did something for its own sake, unconcerned about what it might bring you in the future? For many of us, it is rare to do anything purely for the joy of it, as we are so busy working towards a different life, towards a better future.

As children, we did almost everything for its own sake, except for the things adults imposed on us. If it's not fun for them, my children stop and find something else, and I remember that sense of aimless joy from my own childhood.

As teenagers, this continues to a large extent. Why else do teenagers all over the world spend so much time hanging out with their friends, talking about nothing in particular? They love to do it, so they do it! Many teens also get a great thrill out of doing things they have been told not to, a sense of excitement and rebellion, and this activity too can be done purely for the fun of it.

As adults, we have different roles in the world. We are expected to be responsible, to take things seriously, and this is fine. But when we lose ourselves in those roles, and when we make everything into a quest for future happiness, then we become out of balance with life.

If you look at the world around you carefully, you will see a world that is constantly celebrating and enjoying itself. Animals play, even though the play doesn't seem to serve a 'purpose'. Flowers bloom, thousands more than are needed to ensure their 'future' survival. Everywhere there is growth, joyful expression and beauty.

And if you think of your relationship like a garden, there can be this type of joyful celebration there too, if you learn to keep the future in its proper place.

Make use of the future for practical matters, use it to plan dinner and what you will do on the weekend, then leave it alone and enjoy life, which is always now. Do you ever spend time with a loved one without any end in mind, without trying to 'figure something out' or 'decide on what to do next'? I bet you do, but you may not notice it.

When you have a coffee with a friend, for example, mostly it is entirely purposeless. You are not trying to achieve some future goals, nor are you trying to get something from the other person, you are just enjoying their company in the moment. And when you go walking just to walk, or paint, draw or write, the future disappears. There is only this activity, now.

In intimate relationships, the same principle applies. When you play a game with your loved one, or sit and listen and talk, there can be this sense of play. But beware, thinking will try to take over again and again, turning the interaction into a step along the way, a part of the strategic plan that is moving you closer to that preferred future.

The question to ask in order to find this playfulness is: 'Am I completely present in what I am doing, or am I trying to get something out of it?' If you are completely present, you will notice that you are more aware of your body, and of the sights and sounds arising now. There may be a slowness to your way of being with the other person as you let them finish what they are saying, leave silent spaces between sentences and listen deeply. There might also be spontaneous energy arising, bringing lots of laughter as you joke and play together.

For me, this joy is the undercurrent of all the relationships in my life. There is a sense of laughter, of spontaneity and a sense of fun in almost every interaction. I rarely get lost in the mind's desire to get something from someone else, and when I do, I can feel the difference. And it appears that this lightness is somewhat contagious. Many people I meet start out quite dour and serious, but they become looser and freer as we spend time together.

But mostly, I do this for me. I play because I love it, because I wouldn't live any other way.

Activity – Play For the Sake of It

Arrange to meet with a friend or your partner, purely to catch up and spend some time together. Before you go to meet them, spend a few minutes tuning into your breath and becoming present.

When you meet with the person, act as if you were meeting your favourite person in the world and did not want to miss a moment. See if you can drop future and past completely, leave them alone for the time you are together, and just enjoy being with the person for the sake of it.

Notice how your mind tries to pull you back into 'sensible' matters, how it worries about saying the right thing or getting the best result. Leave it alone! Take the attitude that all is perfect, that all is as it should be, and put your energy into noticing and enjoying the moment instead.

The time you spend may be quiet and peaceful, or it may be raucous and loud, it doesn't matter. What matters is your attention, your alertness and your presence.

Play with play as a way to loosen up your relationships this week. See what happens if you bring a joyful attitude to all your interactions, and most of all, see how it feels to live this way. You won't be disappointed.

Day 2: Enjoying Your Perfection

Your mind thinks there is something wrong with you. In fact, it thinks there are *lots* of things wrong with you and not much time to fix them! With so many things needing fixing in yourself (not to mention your life), it is no wonder that everyone is in such a rush.

As the mind continues its search for problems to fix (that's its main occupation), others enter the line of fire too. Your friends, partner, family and co-workers also need to change a few things, in order for you to be happy. And when will this happiness come? In the future, of course, once every problem is solved. Madness!

And so, almost every human being spends their life stressed and anxious, with brief pauses when they stop thinking about all this for a moment. The stress is created because we are trying to fix something that doesn't exist, never will exist and only ever arises as a thought in our heads – the future. This imagined time leads us to spend our whole lives waiting for something better and trying to create the conditions in which this 'better' will come.

This way of living is a trap, and in relationships it is corrosive and destructive. As soon as you believe that you are not quite perfect, it is a short step to projecting that on to others. Many people aren't aware that this process is happening, they just believe that things need to change!

Luckily for us, others aren't going to change to make us happy. They might change a little, and they might even try hard to meet our demands, but even so, they will never meet the standards of the mind. This is wonderful because it leaves only one person to work with – you.

So then, the mind might say, I need to make a list of all that's wrong with me in order that I can fix it – this is my life's work. Many are on this hamster wheel too, and it leads to the same place, because you will never meet the mind's standards either!

The core of the problem is that you are working on something that doesn't exist – your self-image. The self that the mind criticises and instructs exists as a memory, as a remnant from the past. The change suggested is always based on what you did yesterday, last week or last year, not on what is happening now.

Think about it for a moment and see if this is true.

Activity – Changing Me

Take a pen and, on a piece of paper, make a list of all the things you need to change in your life.

To be happy, I need to . . .

Now make a list of all the non-essentials, things you would like to improve but that aren't as important.

If I have time, I would also like to . . .

Now go back and look at your two lists. Put a line through anything that is based on what you remember yourself doing in the past, anything that isn't based on what is happening this instant.

What is left after you remove the past? Is there anything? If not, then you can simply sit back and enjoy your own perfection.

Your self-image will never be perfect. Even if you get everything 'right', the mind will move the goalposts and there will be something else. A Zen master on his deathbed was asked to describe his life. He replied, 'Just one mistake after another'. That is what life is from the mind's point of view.

But if you drop the attempt to perfect your self-image (which exists only as a thought anyway), then what is left to do? Enjoy yourself. Now!

When you discover who you are beyond thought, beyond that self-image, you will be surprised to know that you are perfect already, that no improvement is possible. Underneath thought, there is open, pure awareness, which you can sense by asking, 'Who is it that is aware of these words?' Ask yourself that and sit without needing to answer it, and you will discover a sense of awareness behind your eyes.

Usually, this awareness is lost in thought. All of our attention is absorbed there, so we don't notice the awareness itself. But if you embrace that awareness as your self, you will find yourself present in this moment, and you will discover that improvement is merely another story.

And yet, you might find yourself exercising, eating well, learning something. Why? Because it's fun! Because you love it! You might find yourself apologising, changing patterns of behaviour, and doing all sorts of things that make your experience of now more pleasant. All of this happens by itself, for the love of what is.

For today, drop all attempts to change yourself or anyone else. Search within yourself for that awareness that you are, and enjoy being that. Then you can be of help to others. Then you can relate from true love. This is your role in this world.

Day 3: Why I Can't Play

When I talk about playfulness in relationships, some people tell me that it makes them feel a little uncomfortable. They are used to protecting themselves, and to making sure all is well and that the relationship is heading along the path they have chosen. The idea of being so open and carefree in relationships is therefore unnerving.

There are two important elements to unpick here. One is about safety and the other is about beliefs and how they block you from living your true nature, out of fear of some disaster.

Let's start with safety. Some people may have tried to take advantage of your innocence or compliance in previous relationships, and therefore the urge to protect yourself is quite natural. But this playfulness I describe is not naive, it is not without assertiveness or boundaries. Indeed, the energy of play is clear, confident and kind. It allows us to move through this world with clarity, kindly explaining to others what we want and moving away from relationships that do not serve us.

Being playful (alert, aware and connected) in your relationships will make you more safe, not less.

Secondly, there are beliefs, those unnoticed, unspoken seeming truths that cause so many problems for human beings. And in relationships, those beliefs usually revolve around fear and desire: the fear of being hurt, or losing something, and the desire to get something. These beliefs drive feelings, which drive behaviour and leave us lost, desperately trying to get what we think we need out of relationships and feeling angry or sad when it doesn't happen.

For example, let's say you are in a new intimate relationship that is exciting and fresh. After a little while, your mind will start to integrate the other person into your story of the future, figuring out what role best suits them and casting them appropriately. Maybe it's the 'happily ever after' story, and so you try to move towards that, seeking a deeper commitment from the other and getting upset if they don't oblige.

And then, when they leave you, there is deep sadness and hurt, because the story, carefully constructed in the mind, no longer seems possible. Your future has been taken away.

In this human world, it seems that many people 'can't' play, because they believe something bad would happen if they did, or because they are busy getting to the future, which doesn't exist.

This isn't a personal fault of anyone's, by the way. It is the way we are as humans. It is also something that is dissolving, which is why this book exists in the first place!

So today, instead of believing those mind stories, let's get them on paper and see if they are true.

Activity – Why I Can't Play

Take a pen and, on a piece of paper or below, finish the following sentences as quickly as you can:

I can't be more playful in my relationships because . . .

If I were more playful then I am sure . . .

Being spontaneous might mean I wouldn't get . . .

Most of all, being playful is risky because . . .

Take a moment to look back at your list. Take your time, spending a minute or two looking at each statement in silence. Don't think about them, just be still and look.

After you have looked at each belief with awareness, close your eyes and imagine what your relationships might be like without the fearful beliefs that keep you from engaging in a playful way with others. Images may come to mind, or it may be a feeling that arises inside. Sit with this for as long as you would like to.

In fact, there is no danger in being a playful participant in the relationships of your life. You are no more likely to get hurt because you are enjoying what is. In fact, you are less likely to be hurt. After all, the mind-identified way of being leads us to want some better future, and most of the hurt we experience occurs when that future fails to arise.

Playfulness has no future. It is a dynamic aspect of mindfulness, of being completely aligned with life as it arises now. This is a much safer place to be, because you can respond to things as they arise instead of being lost in thinking or trying to mould the world into a preconceived idea. When it is unsafe, a safe way to leave will arise, and when someone doesn't respect and honour you, you will find yourself leaving without any effort or drama.

So take some time today to play with your loved ones, and see what your mind says. Bringing those beliefs to the surface will lead to them dissolving, all on their own. Then, you can enjoy your life as it continues to unfold in this wonderful now.

Day 4: Speaking Joyfully and Listening From the Heart

How does speech come, and how do we communicate skilfully? The mind tells us that thinking is needed, that we need to think before we speak and listen carefully, work hard at it. But as we are speaking, the mind is wondering all the while what it means for us, thinking about what to say next and trying desperately to keep on the course it has plotted towards that wonderful land called 'future'.

If I let my mind run the show, I would hardly be listening to you at all! I would be so caught up in mind stuff that I would only gather enough of what you said to be able to keep up. Luckily you would be doing the same, so you probably wouldn't notice my absence.

Speaking to friends in long-term relationships about this book, something keeps coming up, and my friend Janet explained it perfectly. Janet has been in a relationship for more than ten years and she loves her partner deeply, but, as she said, 'We don't listen to each other anymore. When he talks, I'm busy thinking about something else, as if I have heard it all before, and when I speak, I can see that he's not there either.'

These are loving, caring human beings who want the best for each other, and yet, when the mind is running the show, attention can't be held over many years without novelty. The mind is always looking for the new, for the next excitement, so relationships of 10, 20, 50 years are not as interesting to it anymore, unless they are infused with drama.

Mind-based relationships are tiring and need constant newness or at least frequent breaks to survive. Mindful relationships are new every instant, because that is the nature of life if you watch and listen carefully. And watching and listening carefully is one path to not only joyful relationships, but to a joyful life.

These relationship problems arise purely because we believe the talk in our heads, those thoughts that come and go, and believe that's us talking! But if you listen carefully to your loved one, hanging on every syllable without trying to remember it, you will notice two things very quickly.

First, you will notice that thought can cease, or move to the background, and you remain. You are there, watching thought. Second, you will discover that, right now, your partner, friend or whoever you listen to is perfect just as they are. How wonderful!

To play with this practice, I recommend the following simple exercise.

Activity – Listening From the Heart

Go outside today and find somewhere you can sit for a few minutes without being interrupted. Or if this isn't possible, try this activity while walking.

As you sit or walk, take as much of your attention as you can muster to the world of sound. Listen with intensity to every sound that arises.

Don't allow judgements about sounds (good sounds, bad sounds) to take over. Listen to the sounds themselves, not the mind's opinions about them.

Act as if you had never heard before, as if you lived in outer space and only encountered sound for the first time today.

And finally, only pay attention to what you are hearing *now*. As soon as a sound evaporates, leave it alone.

Now try this in a relationship with someone else. Listen intently, without judgement, and only pay attention to what is being said *in this instant*.

Notice what it is like to be there as open, curious attention, instead of as mind stuff.

Thinking is the only barrier to joy, love and delight in relationships. And moving from being predominantly a thinker to being awareness with your loved ones brings profound changes. But the most important difference this makes is for you! It moves you from being this entity, this judging, cynical one who tries to control the world around them, to being a curious, loving person.

I call this 'being you', as this awareness is who you are, not something you achieve through hard work. As you notice who you are underneath all those thoughts, relaxation happens, because you no longer need to deal with all the mind's worries, concerns and demands. There is a sense of freedom in that, a sense of happiness that comes from enjoying the world as it is now.

Then, as this sense deepens, the relationships that remain in your life (some will leave if they're no longer having their stories reinforced) will deepen beyond belief, with playfulness at their core.

But forget about all that, for now. Practise your pure listening today, and see what it is like to be there as awareness, rather than thought. After that, you can choose to keep going down that path, or return to the thinking state.

Day 5: Play-Fighting

As you read this chapter about playful relationships, you may be wondering how this applies when we disagree, when conflict arises in relationships. It appears to the mind that, in this realm at least, there is a need to be serious, to think it through and to protect yourself. Not so!

As it turns out, you can manage seemingly conflictual situations joyfully and playfully too.

Let me be clear, though, I am not talking about any situation in which your safety is at risk. In any such situation, I would recommend getting help from a professional who works in that area.

What I am discussing is the everyday conflicts that human beings experience in relationships. These conflicts can be small things, like the look you give your partner when he didn't clean up after himself, to something bigger, like the discussion of whether to stay married or get divorced. But whether they seem big or small, conflicts have a couple of common elements: the clash of different points of view and the clash of different desires.

Every conflict (in my experience, email me – oli@peacethroughmindfulness.com.au – if I am wrong!) is a clash of opinions, or wishes, or both. You want to go to Spain;

your partner wants to go to Scotland. You believe in helping refugees; your friend does not. I have even seen people argue over whether something was green or blue, and the argument went on for some time!

Take another step back and all of these conflicts are about thoughts. I think Spain is nice; you think Scotland is nice. I think we should help people; my friend has fearful thoughts about people from foreign lands. I think it's green . . . well, you get the idea!

When conflicts arise, they are a great opportunity to loosen up the grip of those thoughts, to play with them rather than taking them seriously. The stronger our grip on those thoughts, the more intense the conflict will be, and the more challenging it might be to step back and be playful. But it is completely possible to bring this energy into those conflicts, and quite often it will dissolve them.

Playfulness is the dynamic aspect of curiosity in some ways. We look with openness and interest, and if thinking doesn't get in the way, we find ourselves celebrating, playing in the now. When conflicts arise in your life, curiosity is a good place to start. Turn your attention inward and see what thoughts are underneath the position you are taking. Of course, your mind will try to convince you that, rather than thoughts, you are holding 'the truth', but look closer and you will see a particular viewpoint and perhaps a desire for something in the future, that's all.

When conflict arises, rather than looking to the other person to change their ways, look inside. See what is driving all this drama, find out the truth of your experience now. Maybe your mind has projected into the future and has an idea of what you 'need'. Then, when someone else (who has their own desires and beliefs) comes at you wanting some other future, your mind feels threatened. Your future happiness is at stake, so it makes sense to fight tooth and nail!

Look closely, though, and look within. Who is the one who holds these beliefs? Who is chasing that future? Where is the self that wants, desires and fears? Can you find it?

When I started looking inside, I was shocked to find that there is no one there. There is a self-image made of thoughts, and there is awareness of that image, but I can't find where this 'I' is located. There is no 'I' that I can point to. There is a body, a perspective and an experience, but no self that I can find. And with no one to protect and serve, I am free to enjoy life, without too many opinions or ideas about how things should be. It's very freeing!

Try the following activity and you will get a feel for what I am describing. You will discover it within yourself.

Activity – Who is Upset?

Close your eyes and bring to mind a conflict in which you were recently involved. Remember as much detail as you can about what happened, especially what happened inside you.

As you sit and recall that event, sit for a moment with each of the following questions, without trying to answer them in the mind. Let the questions sit and *feel* the answer:

- What were you defending? What was this great agitation designed to protect or to get? Were you protecting a belief or trying to get to a better future?

- Who was upset? There were agitated thoughts and emotions arising, but where is the person to whom they belonged?
- And what if you knew there was no separate person there, only a bundle of upset thoughts and emotions? How would you respond to the situation?

Take your time with these questions and try coming back to them during or after a conflict situation. When you get to the heart of these questions, the answers will astound you.

Conflict can become playful when there is no longer a person there 'doing' it. If you feel a strong sense that 'I am being playful', then your mind is running the show. When playfulness takes over, there is no sense of 'I', only the enjoyment of life as it arises. And, in that space, all conflict will dissolve.

Day 6: Playful Connection

Earlier in the week, we played for the sake of it, to loosen up the energy of the relationship you had in focus. Today, we will use playfulness more deliberately, to deepen the connection you feel with those you love. If they want to join in, that's great, and if they don't, that's good too, as this change only requires one.

Connection through the mind is no connection at all. Most human beings try to relate to others this way, through a dense screen of thinking that continually tells you who you are and who the other person is. And as those thoughts roll on and on, there is no possibility of truly seeing that person, of truly hearing what they are saying. Everything is filtered through the thinking mind.

And yet, even in the densest of human experiences, there are breaks. There are moments of spontaneous connection in which the mind is quiet, or at least toned down, and moments of clarity in relationships. This often happens because we are engaged in something that requires intense awareness, or something that doesn't require the participation of the mind.

Sharing these types of experiences together can create a strong bond, as the connection that occurs is deep and unusual. Mind-based relationships lack spark because they are more like deals struck between two minds: 'You be nice to me and agree with what I say and I will do the same . . .'

Think of your dearest friend in the world. Now think about the type of relationship you share. Is it purely based on story? Or are there breaks during which you play in the now together? Any time you laugh and it's not at someone else's expense, this principle is at work. Any time you stop thinking and soak up the beauty of the world around you, it is at work too. And whenever you listen totally to the other, without planning what you will say next, then this nowness is alive in your relationship.

Any relationship that you have voluntarily continued (without the pull of family ties or other coercion) over many years is probably infused with some of this playfulness. But imagine a relationship that is *primarily* based on this type of connection. It is something special.

The basic element of playfulness is attention. And this attention must be directed into what is happening in this instant. If your attention is lost in thought, there is no play. If you are planning what comes next, there is no play. If you are distracted or daydreaming, there is no play.

As a starting point, bring intense awareness to what you see and hear when you are with your loved one. Follow your breath as you spend time together, feel your body against the chair, look closely at your loved one's face, look into their eyes.

As you look at them with this open, curious awareness, you will naturally feel a sense of love, of fondness towards them. This feeling is not the usual mind-based love, which is dependent on the other doing what you want, it is a deeper sense of recognising yourself when you look at the other person, knowing that underneath all their thinking, they are just like you.

This love is quiet, open and alert. It has no opinion about who you should be and it allows you to be yourself in this moment. This is the silent aspect of awareness. Then, out of that silence, something wonderful, enthusiastic and joyful emerges: this playful energy. There is nothing you can do to create it, drag it into the light or to get more of it, but you can offer it an invitation.

Activity – Invitations to Play

Bring a loved one to mind with whom you would like to develop, or deepen, this type of playful connection. When you are next with your loved one, start by being still and alert and listening carefully. As you move into this alertness, you will gradually feel your experience change, from distracted and lost to sharp and focused.

As you sit with your loved one in this focused state, pay

close attention to what is happening now, what they say, what you are doing and what is happening around you.

Allow what you say and do to arise out of this stillness. Let it be spontaneous and playful. This may feel disorienting at first, especially if you are used to planning everything ahead, but give it a try anyway. If it helps, let a good friend know you will be trying this and ask for their support.

Keep with this practice during your time with your loved one and see what happens. Sometimes you may stay in stillness, and sometimes playfulness emerges. Whatever happens, though, will be appropriate to the situation as it arises in this instant.

The mind will say this is dangerous territory, that spontaneity will lead you to act unskilfully (isn't that the mind's job?) and that you will lack heart and compassion. Try it anyway. Your deepest self is pure goodness, pure heart, and no thinking is required to moderate you. The mind needs moderation, yes, but you don't. Be yourself and let playfulness come and all will be well in your world.

Day 7: The Space to Play

There are two competing dimensions in each of us, and the same applies in our relationships, our workplaces, in every aspect of our lives. One dimension is the space of the present moment, a sense of calm and quiet in which things arise and disappear. This space is still, open and relaxed.

Within that dimension, stuff happens, and that 'stuff' is the second dimension. Thoughts arise, emotions arise, events take place and the life show goes on. This dimension in particular wants all of your attention, it wants you to lose yourself in it completely, and this is the human condition.

Many people, and many couples, don't believe they have the space or the time to play, because they are so enthralled with the life show that it is all-pervading. Every moment is absorbed, which really means their attention is absorbed, in thinking, planning, doing. Today is all about bringing this situation into balance.

When you are together with your loved ones, notice the underlying energy of your interactions. Are you generally enjoying yourself and the other's company, or are you trying to get somewhere else? How much of your time together is spent discussing the past and the future? Is there a playfulness there, or does it feel serious, or gossipy, or flat? The answers to these questions will give you some clues about which dimension predominates.

Over time, when time and mind dominate, relationships either become flat and lifeless or they survive on a sort of nervous energy as you pull apart the past and plan for the future. But all this can change in an instant.

Activity – Becoming Spacious

There is a simple way to experiment with this shift: simply watch for tension, anxiety, worry or other negative emotions arising within your relationships. And when those feelings arise, use them as a reminder to become very present, very focused on what is happening in this instant. Listen closely to the other person and, whatever they are saying, make this instant your primary focus. Watch for the mind's attempts to sidetrack you and to grab that attention back, and keep returning to now, now, now!

Don't try to change your responses to the other person, let them happen as they do, but watch more closely than before, notice the way you speak, the way they speak and what you are focused on together.

As you become still in this watchful space, feel the openness that is there when you aren't trying to get anywhere. Listen to the silence between sounds when the other person speaks, enjoy the silence between thoughts as your mind ebbs and flows and sense yourself as the watcher of all that happens now.

There is a playfulness to this space that is gentle, calm and quiet, and it is inseparable from who you are underneath all that mind stuff. Play with it today and see what happens next.

The old way, living through the mind, is almost completely conditioned, and those who have known you for years will probably be able to predict how you will respond to different situations. In some ways, the mind is like a machine, giving back similar outputs to similar inputs. As beliefs change over time, the outputs change too, of course, but there is not much variability or creativity there. Not much space to play.

Awareness (which is you), free of the thrall of mind, has enormous freedom. Imagine all the options available to you if you didn't have any beliefs about what you should do, nor any hopes or fears for the future.

Often, our relationships are shaped and manicured by these beliefs and hopes. In my own experience, the search for approval was such a driver in my relationships that I was constantly checking and fine-tuning myself, keeping certain aspects of me hidden and highlighting the nicer ones. This is a bit like plastic surgery for your personality, except that it keeps happening! It was exhausting and stressful, but I believed at the time that it was the path to future happiness, so it continued.

When it struck me that most of what I thought of as 'my relationships' actually happened only in my head (through thinking), I was so relieved! Now, all that is left is the interaction I am having now, and in the space this opens up, everything becomes playful.

When I tell people about this way of being, they sometimes say, 'I'll try to remember that.' But don't try to be different, and please don't try to remember! That's more thinking, after all. Just notice. Become aware of what is happening inside you as you relate to others and watch the quality of the relationship closely. As you watch, awareness will naturally transform the way you relate as the old pattern dissolves. What is left after all that old stuff goes is you, so how could you remember to be it?

Today I invite you to experiment with these simple changes in one of your relationships. Bring awareness to your interactions, notice yourself as that spacious awareness and see what arises within the relationship. It always amazes me how so small a change can make such a profound difference.

WEEK 4

Letting Them Be

When relationships are seen through thinking, they become a means to an end, a way to achieve certain life goals. These goals might include 'being good enough', 'being appreciated' or 'being loved', and although they seem like reasonable aims from the mind's perspective, trying to get these things from outside yourself is a dangerous game.

Relationships that are primarily there to make you feel a certain way or reassure your ego that your self-image is good enough can easily become manipulative, complicated and stressful. And, even worse, this way of relating leads us to put others in charge of our happiness, and blame them for our disappointment, upset and sadness when our demands aren't met.

As soon as I expect you to do or say certain things in order for me to be happy, I am in a trap and at your mercy. This is both dangerous for me (because who knows what you will do) and unfair for you. Understandably it tends to lead to resentment, frustration and fear, because we are at the mercy of other people who are busy chasing what they want.

And yet, through all this confusion, many relationships are infused with joy, delight and peace, at least some of the time. The light of awareness penetrates even through thick conditioning and mind stuff, which is what makes living life bearable!

But rather than having dense, stressful relationships with glimpses of enjoyment, or relationships that only satisfy you if others 'do the right thing', this week I will show you how to transform your experience so that the opposite is true. By making a small change in focus, you can instead enjoy relationships that are fun and peaceful, with glimpses of drama and mind-related problems. And all it takes is a quick 180-degree turn.

Day 1: Owning It

If you have ever watched another person and worried about whether they liked what you said or did, hoping they will give you a positive response, then you know how draining the search for approval tends to be. Having spent a couple of decades with approval-seeking as my religion, I experienced this stress on a daily (or maybe hourly) basis.

Looking back, I can see what was happening, but at the time I had no idea. I was lost in the process. Back then, I thought the following was going on:

1) I needed certain things in order to be happy, especially to be good enough in the eyes of others, to be loved and to be approved of.

2) I knew what approval and loved looked like, and if other people did or said certain things, then I would know that I was alright.
3) In order to get other people to do and say those things, I needed to improve myself in certain ways, becoming funnier, kinder, more peaceful, etc.
4) When that approval didn't come, it was either because I was a terrible person (cue sad overture) or because *they* were mean and nasty (cue sinister overture). The answer was either to work hard to change me (in the future) so I was better, or to work hard to change them (in the future) so they would do as they should.

It's no wonder life was a bit stressful. When I look now with clarity and peace, I can see that there was something else going on:

1) I was lost in thought.
2) Those thoughts said I could find happiness in the future if certain conditions were met.
3) To meet those conditions, I tried to get others to say and do certain things.
4) When there was a gap between what my mind wanted and what happened, I felt stress and blamed the world for it.

My attention was drawn into thought, completely lost, and those thoughts directed me to look for contentment outside, through getting certain things. Without those things, I believed that happiness was impossible (we all have needs, after all). So I set the trap, fell into it and then felt sorry for myself because I was stuck. And it all happened in my head.

Then, one day, I wondered: what if I made it my own responsibility to find peace? What if I cut others out of the equation and looked for peace within instead? I realised that every ounce of stress was caused by believing thoughts, and I started looking within when I felt upset, instead of looking around for someone to blame.

Let me be clear, though, I didn't start blaming myself for the stress I experienced, I just started looking inside to find out what on earth was going on. And in this simple shift, from looking out and blaming to looking in and owning it, everything started to change.

You see, when you start to use the disappointments and dissatisfaction as a reminder to look inside and see what is happening, you start to learn all sorts of things. You start to see that all unhappiness arises in the mind and that it is always a story of the past. This past includes what happened ten seconds ago, as well as ten years ago. It's gone. The mind wants to keep it alive because it strengthens your self-image and gives the mind something to do, but learn to let it be and you will immediately feel better.

And by taking responsibility for dealing with what arises in you, another layer of stress will drop, because you will no longer be feeding the mind's stories of victimhood. The energy that went into thinking can then be focused on what *is* instead. Here is a simple activity to show you how to begin this process.

Activity – Owning It

Close your eyes for a moment and remember something you experienced recently that led to feelings of stress and negativity. It could be small or large, but make it an event that still brings up those feelings when you remember it.

As you recall that event and those sensations start to arise in your body, take your attention away from the memory and put it on to the sensations. Leave the past alone and work instead with what is arising now, the feelings in your body.

As you explore those feelings with your attention, ask yourself, 'Who is upset? Who is experiencing this now?' and sit still without needing to answer the questions.

Take the attitude that what is inside you is yours to experience, and that what others do or say is up to them. Make your only job the experiencing of what is.

And finally, as you make this 180-degree shift, notice how it feels to take full responsibility in this way. The mind may say that it will be painful, or scary, but is it really?

Leaving stories alone frees up attention to invest elsewhere, and if you use that attention to become friendly with what is, then your experience will fundamentally change. All the energy you used to spend mentally complaining, or trying to figure out how to get others to change, becomes fuel for knowing yourself.

Uncompromisingly turn within, whenever something seems to go wrong in life, and you will be glad that you took on this responsibility, not for what others say and do but for what is arising in you. Who else will take care of this if not you?

Day 2: Loving Me First

Often, in relationships, our tendency is to pay attention mostly to the other, to what they say and do and how this compares to what the mind says they should say and do. We focus our energy, our love, primarily on others, hoping that they will reciprocate in the way we want, and that this will lead us to happiness in the future.

Predictably, this leads to problems, as we are investing our energy in someone else in the hope that they will do as we would like. Other people, though, are concerned primarily with what they are trying to achieve in life, and are often unaware of what we want from them.

And even if they do comply, the happiness we feel is dependent on this continuing, meaning that we can place too much responsibility in the hands of another. Life being as it is (unpredictable), this person may leave, change or even die, leaving us with the sense that our happiness has gone too.

All of this makes relationships, and life, unnecessarily messy, but there is another, simpler way to live. Love yourself first.

Before we explore this too deeply, let me be clear what I mean by love. I don't mean saying nice things about someone. I don't mean thinking nice thoughts about someone. And I don't mean doing nice things for someone. These may all be expressions of love, but they are not love.

From my perspective, love is the complete acceptance of the other exactly as they are now. To love is to look at someone without thinking, to listen without judging, to be aware of them without trying to change them in any way.

Out of that space of allowing, all kinds of words, actions, even thoughts, may flow or not, it doesn't matter. The love is the spacious attention itself, so whether it leads to action or not is less important than the fact that it *is* in the first place.

What we normally call love is a story. It's a belief that 'I love you', based on who I believe you are, what I remember you doing in the past and how that relates to my own self-image. It's all a mind game. Underneath that thinking, it may be that you have looked at the person with acceptance and love, but then the mind comes in and complicates things.

Love is the expression of who you are, and it isn't dependent on another person or on certain events. And when you learn to look without thinking, this love flows into the world freely and easily, but you must start with yourself.

Activity – Loving Me

Take a few minutes to close your eyes and notice yourself without judgement. When I say 'yourself', I don't mean what you did yesterday or last week, I don't mean your self-image, I don't even mean your body. I mean you, the one who experiences all this, the one who is aware of the things that happen and the thoughts that arise.

Move attention to your breath and feel it flowing in and out gently. There is no need to make your breath deeper or shallower, just allow breath to come and go and watch it.

Feel what is happening in your body and allow that to be as it is too. Curiously explore what is with your attention.

And finally, allow whatever thoughts are there in your awareness now to be there, just let them be. See if you can smile at them without getting lost in them or trying to change them. Spend a few minutes sitting and watching.

Sitting in this openness and looking at what is arising without making it into a story is itself love. You are completely allowing your experience to be as it is right now, which is a caring thing to do.

We all seem to be searching for some kind of 'unconditional' love, and when you look upon your inner world without judgement, this is what you are giving to yourself. Your mind will look upon it and say, 'Well, I *could* love it, if only the thoughts were nicer, if only the body were thinner, if only . . .' and these 'if onlys' will go on for a lifetime if you let them.

But unconditional love is in you, *is you,* right this moment. And when you begin to look upon yourself without judging what *is*, this unconditional love is free to move within. Strangely enough, once this movement starts, you will find your judgements about other people starting to dissipate and dissolve, not because they become 'better' or 'nicer', but because you stop thinking about who they are and what it all means.

This is the most joyous way to be in a relationship with others and yourself, to experience that relationship only in this instant, and to let it unfold exactly as it does right now. In fact, we don't have a choice about this – everything happens this instant and it happens exactly as it does, and to resist it is painful.

Once you become comfortable in this space of open looking, you begin to have some choice about whether you resist or allow. And when you feel the difference between these two approaches to life, that choice will start to make itself.

Day 3: Loving Them Next

Love in relationships is usually quite delicate. It depends on the right conditions and is easily destroyed, or so it seems. When I use the term 'love' here, I don't only mean romantic love, I mean that feeling of goodwill and friendliness you feel towards people in your life, be they friends, colleagues, family, or the person who runs the post office.

This sense of love is often conditional, in that it is supported by thoughts about the past, and those thoughts determine whether we feel positive about someone or not. I was talking to my friend the other day and she was telling me about someone in her life, describing what they said to her and trying to figure out what it meant. 'I can read energy', she told me, 'and I could feel that something wasn't right.'

As we kept talking, something became clear: her mind was trying to figure out if that person liked her. If not, she would not like them either, because the mind doesn't want to be the *only* one who loves, it doesn't want to be vulnerable.

Yesterday, we explored how to truly love yourself without conditions, and today we will expand this to see how the practice of loving others without conditions can bring you deeper into the present moment, but there *is* one condition . . .

The love I describe here has nothing to do with thought, belief or past experience. It has nothing to do with what that person might do in the future. And what does that leave?

It leaves us loving the person in front of us *right now* unconditionally, then leaving them alone mentally once the bodies move apart. This is a radical shift.

If you look at most of what you call 'my relationships', you will probably discover that they are imagined, they happen inside your head. You speak to someone for an hour and then spend the next month reliving the conversation in your mind. You spend hours wondering what the person meant, whether they like you and even planning future conversations. This isn't love, it's just more thinking.

True love has nothing to do with what your mind says. It is the experience of being with the other in a state of complete allowing, letting them be as they are now. But this is easier said than done for most of us.

After all, how do you allow someone to be difficult, angry, aggressive or depressed? How can you stay loving when someone is negative about you, themselves or the world? There are two steps to take to move in this direction, and they are both surprisingly simple.

The first step is to make the distinction between your experience and theirs. Often we try to change others because *we* feel uncomfortable around them when they do or say certain things. We end up trying to control them so that we don't have to experience that feeling. Leave their experience alone and go deeper into yours. If you feel uncomfortable, experience that fully, stay alert and present and watch that sensation arise and fall. Go back to Day 1 of this week and own your inner experience.

The second step takes a bit more practice, but is also quite simple, and I call it 'Looking Beyond'.

Activity – Looking Beyond

Usually when we experience an event, the mind slaps a label on it as quick as can be and we stop looking. We don't see past that label. When another person is being rude, the mind might label them, saying, 'She's so rude, I can't believe she . . .' and then the story rolls on.

What we are looking at here is the person's conditioning, not the person. Their true self is hiding underneath all the compulsive behaviour driven by thoughts and feelings, and if you can look *through* that conditioning, you will see someone very different.

Try this when you are out in the world having interactions that don't require much attention, for example at the supermarket or while sitting on a bus. Start by closing your eyes and feeling yourself breathe. Use the awareness of breath to take some attention out of thought and put it into life, now. Feel yourself becoming present as you make this shift.

Open your eyes again and go about your day, but whenever you see another person, look into their eyes and see the light of awareness shining back. See that they have the same watcher there underneath all the thinking that goes on. You don't need to stare or freak anybody out, but look into their eyes for a moment as you pass through their lives.

Practise this 'looking beyond' in these simple everyday situations and then see if you can expand it to the people you spend more time with. As you watch them, notice the light of awareness there in their eyes, and make this more interesting than their conditioning.

This simple change has the power to radically transform your relationships. More importantly, if you practise it, you will find yourself drawn deeper and deeper into the present moment as all resistance to what is starts to dissolve. All this is possible because you looked deeper than the behaviours that are there on the surface.

Day 4: Letting Them Speak

The mind is so powerful when we identify with it. It drives our behaviour, dictates our beliefs and determines what we say and do. As you continue your journey of moving from mind-identified living to living in the moment, you will see how this spell can be broken through practice and observation, and yet, most people remain at the mercy of the thoughts they experience.

So, when our loved ones speak, it is no surprise that often what is being spoken is not their deepest truth, but a reflection of thought. Depending on what those thoughts are, that speech may be loving and kind (to a point), or it may be self-centred and negative. If the words of our loved ones seem charged with negative energy, something within us can become activated. This, of course, is the thinking mind, which loves to resist, to argue, to make others wrong. This is how it survives.

After all, that thinking mind, that idea of yourself as a separate person, can only continue to appear real by defining itself (yourself) as different from other people. By drawing lines between you and your loved one, it strengthens the illusion of separateness. If you look closely inside, you will see that resistance and making others wrong solidifies your sense of identity. This is easy to see in groups with shared beliefs, who often define themselves as much by pointing out how the 'others' are 'wrong' as they do by celebrating their own stories. Religions, political movements and other groups built around shared belief mostly tend to do this.

This is nothing personal, of course. It is a part of the human condition. When your loved one speaks and your mind disagrees, it is merely resistance arising, it doesn't belong to anyone in particular. But if you get lost in that resistance, if you argue, disagree, or emotionally react to what they are saying, you go deeper into the world of thinking, deeper into the mind-identified life. And we have tried that. It isn't fun.

This old way of doing things makes us harder, more defined, seemingly solid. It also feeds negative thinking and resistance, making life feel more like a battle for survival than a fun game. And, of course, it isn't the only option; there is a more peaceful way to live.

If you practise the art of not taking others' speech personally, something amazing happens. Instead of feeling offended, angry and negative when someone else is criticising you, or being negative themselves, you can be there as the witness. You can simply watch, listen and allow, without needing to do or say anything, without needing to get involved.

As a starting point, all you need to do is make a small attitude shift. Normally, we act as if what others think, feel and say is important to us, and if it doesn't line up with our worldview, we get ready to fight. The alternative is to act as if what others think, feel and say is important to *them* and that it is our job to hear and acknowledge it.

This is a profound change that frees you from the need to change the mind of anyone, ever, and you can try it out with this simple little activity.

Activity – Being Space

Normally, when we listen, the mind is active. We mentally reinforce what we believe to be true, and when the other contradicts this, we are ready to pounce.

Today, I invite you instead to be the space for what is said, to allow it to arise and disappear in your awareness without mentally or verbally arguing with it.

Take a moment first to listen to the sounds around you now. There may be birds, cars, people or other sounds happening in your awareness. Just listen. Allow those sounds to come and go as they please, without needing to label them as 'good' or 'bad' or 'this' or 'that'. Listen.

As you listen in this way, notice how the sounds arise in awareness and disappear, without leaving a trace. When the mind argues with or labels those sounds, this is a trace of the past; the sound is gone, but the mind holds on to its echo. Being the space means allowing the sound that arises in this instant, then leaving it be.

Now take this experiment into an interaction with another person. Pick a simple interaction to start with, and as the other person speaks, see if you can sense the words *and* the awareness that listens. Pay attention to what arises, and to yourself at the same time.

Make it your job to be the space for those words, and leave the other person to work with their own thoughts and beliefs. And whenever something is triggered, some resistance to what is, don't act it out, don't argue, just experience that resistance, that negativity, also arising in the space of your awareness. Be the space for that too. Allow everything, and make your inner experience the main focus of your attention.

There is something incredibly freeing about putting down the imagined responsibility for the thoughts, beliefs and feelings of others. Surprisingly, this leaves you more available to be there for your loved ones, to help them think things through and to support their growth. But instead of dictating that growth, you become like the rain, gently nourishing without trying to do anything.

And this experience, this way of being, is infused with the peace that comes when you know that the other's experience isn't yours to process, that instead you can be there and watch.

Day 5: Letting Conflict Be

For most people, when conflict arises within relationships, it brings with it some uncomfortable feelings. Sometimes this conflict may involve you directly, or it may be happening around you, for example when two family members disagree, or when work colleagues don't get along.

Because of the feelings these situations give rise to, our first response is often either to do something to stop the conflict or to escape. And, as you will read today, there is nothing wrong with the attempt to do either of these. It is fine to walk away when others are arguing (or find another job where the team gets along better). It is also fine to help people to end their conflict if you can. But if you can take these paths from a position of *allowing* rather than resistance, then you can be at peace regardless of the outcome and, as a handy side effect, you will be more effective if and when an opportunity to help arises.

If we start by allowing what is, and then see what the moment offers us, we can take action, or not, in a peaceful way.

Better than this, though, are the opportunities to practise *with* those uncomfortable feelings rather than trying to change them or run away, as we have been taught to do.

After all, this is the primary resistance to your inner experience. The outside world is not as important as what happens inside you, as you can observe when you watch closely. If, for example, you see two people arguing on a reality TV show, it's less likely to bring up negative feelings, and you may even find yourself enjoying the show! But if those two people are *your* parents, and the argument is in *your* lounge, then your relationship to what's happening changes completely, and some form of inner resistance is likely to arise.

Resistance works like this: first, a feeling arises that the mind doesn't like. The mind seeks the cause of the feeling, blames it on the situation happening either here and now or in the mind (in the past). The mind then sets to work trying to remove the cause by changing the situation, to prevent it happening again or somehow protect you from its impact. The mind's efforts then stay focused on the outside world and on planning your responses to that world so that no further feelings arise.

Racism is a clear example of this principle at work. If someone feels uncomfortable around people from unfamiliar places or cultures, their mind may try to avoid that discomfort by keeping to places where people from that person's country and culture spend time. Some minds also campaign to stop more people from unfamiliar places coming to live in 'their' country. Why? Because then they don't have to deal with the feelings that arise. So, when you see racism, know that it's not that person doing it, it's a mind pattern that happens to you too.

Activity – Shifting Attention

The underlying assumption of the mind in these scenarios is that the world outside needs to change and that there must be something wrong with the present moment. Or, more accurately, there was something wrong with the past, because by the time the mind has chewed an event over, it is long gone.

Let's start with a different assumption. Let's assume that life gives you exactly what you need at exactly the right moment. Notice how whenever you breathe in, the right mix of oxygen and carbon dioxide is there. See the ground that is unfailingly there every time you step, and every time you fall, always there to hold you.

Of course, when some uncomfortable feeling arises, the mind's first question is: 'What's been happening out there? Why am I feeling this?'

Don't let this question direct your attention though. Ask yourself instead: 'What's happening inside me? What do I feel this instant?'

Forget about why it's there, what caused it or what would prevent it from arising in the so-called future. Direct your attention inside. Feel it directly. Become present.

Use the sensations arising inside to draw your attention within. Notice what is there, see how it moves or doesn't, and be still as the watcher of it.

Feel your breath coming and going as you watch, and explore your inner world with a gentle curiosity.

Congratulations, you have found freedom from conflict!

Once you are back as the observer instead of the thinker, some actions may arise, but they will come from a different place. Instead of acting out of negativity and resistance, you will find yourself doing what seems best in the present moment, free from the past.

But more important than the action you take, or even the experiences you have, is the uncompromising attitude of looking within for answers first. Whenever a problem arises, leave the outside world alone (with your attention, anyway) and find out what is arising inside.

Work with that world, and real change is possible, real freedom is possible. Let the world around you do its thing, free from your mind's interference.

And when you live from *that* position, life starts to take care of itself.

Day 6: The Deepest Connection

Within almost every human being there seems to be a deep desire for connection. When this desire is projected outwards, we seek it through relationships, through approval. If this desire is turned inward, however, something different starts to happen, and that is the subject of our journey today.

When we try to connect with other people, it often seems that an effort is required. We need to try to be like this or like that, to listen well and think of kind things to do. This type of connection is fragile and conditional, because it is based on an unspoken deal: if I'm nice to you and you're nice to me, then we'll stay friends, or partners, or whatever. And when two people with two different sets of thinking, beliefs and conditioning look at this bargain from two different points of view, their idea of who is being nice and who isn't may not quite match up!

Even when this type of connection functions fairly well, it feels more like a contract than love, although there may be moments of joy and lightness in the partnership. If you want the relationship to be based on joy and lightness, though, you need to start from a different vantage point.

The difficulty with this outward movement, which is the basis of 'normal' human relationships, is that there is an inbuilt sense that something 'out there' will bring you to completeness and happiness. This flows on to a sense that the other person's job in the relationship is to move you a little closer to this happiness, which of course is *going to* occur in the future.

If we follow this back even further we can see that all of this is grounded in the belief that something is wrong with you and with your life now, and that something needs to change or be added or taken away for you to be OK.

And if you start from the belief in incompleteness, then any relationship will have a needy, anxious quality at times, maybe all the time. After all, if you have invested your future happiness in the other person's hands, you are going to want to have some control over what they do. And what is the other person doing? Exactly the same!

What if we started from the opposite view instead? What if you discovered (not believed) that you were already completely perfect? From that discovery, and from your true self, connections begin to have a different quality, and you can get a taste of this by doing a little experiment in your daily life.

Activity – Starting From Completeness

Close your eyes for a moment and feel your body breathing. Don't try to change anything about the breath, just feel it.

As your attention moves deeper into the present moment, watch the thoughts arising in your mind, allowing them to come and go in their own time. Don't get involved with them, just notice.

Now feel your body from the inside. Notice the sensations that are arising and let every one be, just be curious with it.

As you watch all these things arising – sensations, thoughts, images, movements – you may notice that there are two levels of experience. There is stuff arising and there is awareness of that stuff arising. Which one is you?

Are you the owner of those transient thoughts? Are you the body? The emotions? Or are you the watcher of all that?

And if you sense that you are the awareness watching it all, feel that awareness and notice how it doesn't have any opinions, desires or needs. It is completely perfect already. Don't just believe these words, though. Go inside and *feel* what is true for you.

Practise noticing this awareness as the constant background of your life, and then see what happens when you start from this platform in your relationships. Live from this inner stillness, allow the connection to arise in this moment, and know that you don't need anything from outside to complete you.

Relationships based in awareness have a fundamentally different set of principles from those that are based in the mind.

Connecting through the mind is based in time, in that the relationship is kept alive by thinking about what happened after the fact, while connecting through awareness always happens right now.

Connecting through the mind, we are mostly interested in what happens and what it means for us, so the events, words and thoughts are of great importance. Connecting through awareness, we are mostly interested in the inner space out of which everything arises, so the words, events and thoughts are allowed to come and go without disturbing us.

And finally, connecting through the mind is based on the desire for completeness, so every action is in some way aimed at getting this 'me' closer to 'my goals'. Connecting through awareness, we already know ourselves to be complete and perfect (even if we don't always notice it!) and our only desire is to move deeper into that completeness. Therefore we can be there, completely available for the other person without needing them to act according to a certain set of mind rules.

This change has another deeper benefit, though. Beyond the relationship improvements, it can heal the split that is in you now, the split between 'what is' and 'what I want', and the split between 'who I am' and 'who I think I am'.

Wholeness and perfection are your natural state, and all you need to do is to look for these within.

Day 7: Allowing Space and Silence

Many relationships, like many lives, go from one thing to another, non-stop. There is conversation, decision-making and shared activity. There are things to do, places to go and, of course, plenty to talk (and think) about. Such relationships go up and down (in the minds of those involved) based on what happens between the people involved, and when this activity starts to slow, many relationships break down as the mind seeks out what is new and exciting.

The mind judges the value of a relationship by examining what comes out of it, what you 'get' from it, and for the mind to be getting something, things need to be happening. At the beginning of relationships, when everything is new and you are getting to know each other, this is easy, but try living with someone for 15 years and see how many new, exciting stories you have to share! They say that familiarity breeds contempt, but this is only the case if you are lost in thought.

After all, this 'familiarity' only exists as a story that is held together by the belief in time. If there is only now, and if you interact with a loved one without looking to the memories the mind holds, without thinking at all, then everything is fresh and new. The only reason it feels stale is because the mind is there, directing your attention, telling you, 'This is boring. You've heard it all before.'

Free from the hypnosis of mind, the silence that begins to arise in relationships is refreshing, complete and enjoyable. The stillness of sitting together without doing anything in particular is so full and so joyful, that there is nothing to do and no one to become. And yet, out of this silence and stillness, new things seem to spring, new ideas, new adventures, new conversations.

In the ordinary, mind-identified state, these conversations and adventures are what matters most. When we practise mindfulness, what matters most is being yourself, looking upon the world as awareness, without thinking about and judging what you see and experience. From this view of the world, staying connected with your true nature, which is itself stillness and silence, is the most important thing you can do, and all else flows out of that connection naturally. Relationships become effortless and enjoyable when you put your attention and energy into noticing that still, quiet place and let words and actions flow out of that as they will.

If your relationships are mostly mind-identified, you might be wondering how on earth such a thing is possible, or it may sound like some superhuman act of will. Luckily, though, there are some simple ways to experiment with this way of being with others, and one experiment I particularly enjoy I call 'Noticing Stillness'.

Activity – Hearing Silence, Noticing Stillness

Silence and stillness are already there in your interactions with others. Every encounter is a blend of sound and silence, activity and stillness, but this isn't usually noticed because the mind is in control and it can only think about things (words, events, objects). Try sitting in silence and thinking about that silence. How would you describe it? What would you call it? There's not much for the mind to play with there!

When all is quiet, the mind gets busy thinking, analysing, comparing and projecting, as otherwise it starts to fade.

But today I invite you to try something a little bit different: when there are gaps in your conversation with another person, instead of thinking about the next thing, listen intently to the silence itself. Listen wholeheartedly, as if the silence were as important as the words.

And at the same time, when there is no need for you to be active in the conversation, either because the other person is speaking or because no one is speaking, be still and feel your body from the inside. Listening will still happen, of course, but you can quite easily feel your breath and feel how still your body is sitting while allowing your brain to make sense of the words.

Notice any silent gaps arising in yourself as you sit and listen. Are there spaces between the arising of thoughts? If so, notice that inner quiet, and if not, keep feeling the body and listening to the silence in the conversation.

You have to be alert when you practise this. The gaps between words and sentences may be short as the other speaks, but they will be there, otherwise you wouldn't be able to distinguish the words from each other. And when there is a longer pause, resist the urge to fill it straight away. Be still, stay present, and see what arises spontaneously.

You can still speak while practising this, and you can fully participate in the conversation. Remain aware of the stillness and the silence at the same time, and allow the rest to take care of itself.

The mind believes that relating in this way will reduce your effectiveness, or make you less interesting, but the opposite is true. As you relate to other people from this alert, quiet space, the tendency to be thinking about something else as the other is talking drops. And without this mind stuff to get in the way, you will hear clearly and respond out of a clear understanding of what was said. The mind doesn't help in these situations; it is in your way. Try relating without using it as your primary tool, and you will see how easy it is to get along in this world.

WEEK 5

Living the Journey

This week, as our journey continues, we will explore the practical application of the lessons in this book and the practice of mindfulness in some of life's most challenging places. These tend to be the places that we as humans try to avoid, but they are also the source of our deepest learnings and most profound growth, if we can embrace them. This week you will discover that it is possible to be simultaneously kind and assertive, accepting and straight, even when those around you are acting out their conditioning in ways that push your buttons!

Each day of this week takes a different view on those challenges and presents an alternative way of working with what arises, and although it may seem as if they are instructions on living mindfully, they are actually pointers, telling you to look within, to return to you.

We begin the week by exploring the common challenge of what to do when those around you are not coping well with this thing called life. Should you run away? Tell them to snap out of it? Or maybe ignore the whole thing? Or can you be there and allow the whole thing to take care of itself? Let's find out.

Day 1: Responding With Silence

In my daily life, I often find myself in the company of someone who is speaking or acting out their conditioning. By this I mean they are speaking as if some belief in their head is the truth, and as if life contradicting that belief is an act of war. This often looks like yelling, cross words, angry tones, accusing statements or general complaining.

As someone who has always tried to keep the peace, these happenings are like a fish hook dripping with juicy bait and sometimes there is nothing I want more than to get on-board and try to fix things. And this never, ever works.

Whenever I get involved in these situations and try to sort them out, I notice that they get worse. Others get more annoyed, and I can be drawn into following suit, so before long, there is no one calm in the room and all is chaos and noise.

A few years ago, I decided to try something different. I decided to make it my job to listen and understand but not to fix, suggest or interfere (unless my kids are attacking each other, of course). I decided to respond with silence.

A friend recently said to me that silence is not the absence of sound, it is the absence of that plotting, scheming thinker who routinely takes over our mouths and our bodies, and this is the silence I am describing. It's not that I don't speak, but that I let the speech arise naturally as I watch and listen.

For example, my son Liam is a sensitive soul, and sometimes he gets upset over things that adults see as minor events. When people try to convince him that the event is minor, all hell breaks loose and he gets even more upset. But when I sit next to him and listen, without getting drawn into the story in any way, he settles down quite quickly. I allow the space for the emotion to move and it does.

In fact, this sounds like I'm more active than I am. I don't even *allow the space,* I just stay out of the way and don't stir the pot. The active part is being alert and listening and watching carefully, active awareness rather than active mind.

It seems that this way works well in other situations too: when a friend has a problem, or when a work colleague has had enough of the politics. And it works because each of them has the solution, *their solution*, there already, they just can't see it through all that mind stuff. In the silence, there is no one to feed the thinking and everything becomes calmer, slower and more effective. Then, before you know it, they are on their way once more.

But secretly, I don't do this for them, I do it for me. When you sit in that silence and listen, just being there, there is a deepening sense of peace, a return of your attention to your inner world. You can be present with the person and deepen your mindfulness, all while helping them solve their problem without actually doing anything to help. Now that is a magic trick worth perfecting!

Activity – Becoming a Mirror

Try this next time someone comes to you with a problem or has a problem while you are present and see what it feels like, as well as what happens around you.

Watch and listen carefully to what is happening, but not with the intent to change it, only with curiosity, as if you were watching a movie or a play, deeply engaged but not trying to write the script.

Breathe as you watch, feel the breath and use it to stay present.

Allow thoughts about the situation and what to do to come and go. You can come back to them later if you need them, but for now, watch closely instead.

If someone asks you a question, answer it honestly, even if the answer is 'I don't know'. Otherwise, don't speak or intervene unless someone is unsafe. Just watch.

As you watch, sense the awareness that is taking it all in, the awareness that you are. Be there as that, not as a little mind with opinions and complaints, be the watcher.

After the situation dissolves or you move on, see if you can stay there as the watcher for the rest of the day.

Our minds like to believe that it all depends on us, that without our intervention, the world around us will collapse somehow. But how do you keep the sun in the sky? How do you maintain gravity at the right level? You don't? Oh!

Then perhaps the world is taking care of itself, in spite of your efforts to mould it. Perhaps life is on top of the details, like the director in the movie you watched. If this is the case, then all we need to do is to become this open, aware watcher and enjoy the show. Of course, you will still do things, you are a part of the show after all!

But today, for a few hours, I invite you to let life take care of it, to be there as the witness of it, and to see whether all that mental figuring out was ever necessary.

Day 2: Celebrating Difference

The mind is a fan of conformity, of neat rows with rational orderly things in their correct places. Perhaps this makes us feel safe, because we have the illusion of predictability. And so, our minds create the 'perfect' image of the world as it 'should' be, showing us the blueprint for our happiness.

In many relationships, this gets translated into what our partners 'should' or 'shouldn't' do. Your mind develops a clear set of rules and regulations by which the other person needs to abide in order to be the perfect partner. They may not know these rules, but they should (says the mind)!

Unfortunately, being the perfect partner is not on most people's to-do list. They have their own hopes, dreams and goals, and if you were honest about your list of demands, they might reconsider the whole thing!

Your partner has a list for you too, of course, and you might notice that you missed an item on the list when they get angry or upset with you. Do you want to spend your days trying to fulfil those commandments?

What if, instead of seeking conformity, we could celebrate the differences between us? What if we could appreciate the quirks of each other in the same way that we appreciate the sunset, or the storm clouds rolling in? This is possible, and it only requires one thing.

That one thing is a shift from knowing to curiosity, something that is incredibly powerful. To be curious about something, you have to be interested, aware and alert. You have to be more interested in looking and learning than in judging, and you have to watch and listen closely.

Of course, the 'you' I am talking to is not the mind, is not the self-image. The self-image can't watch and listen because it's an image, it doesn't actually exist! And the thinking mind is merely a bundle of words and pictures floating through awareness. So, when I refer to you, I am referring to that awareness.

There are many ways to step into this open, curious awareness, and my favourite is simply to stop labelling everything. When objects are seen or heard, the mind labels them at lightning speed, creating a world as it tells you that this is a tree, that he is your husband, that that is the sound of the train. All of this is so normal that it isn't noticed, but those labels stop you from looking and listening truly, because once you know what it is, it doesn't require further attention. This is the knowing that we need to move past if we want to experience the world as it is.

Activity – No Labels

Close your eyes for a moment and bring your attention within. Imagine that you have stepped into a strange land where nothing is familiar, and your job is to take in as much as you can.

Open your eyes and spend a few minutes exploring your surroundings. Look upon and listen to everything without calling it anything or commenting on it mentally. See if you can be curious about what is here now.

If labels do arise, keep looking anyway, notice as much as you can about each thing that is here, and leave the mind alone.

Notice the habit of moving back into the midstream and the addictive nature of that. And when that arises, come back to the now, and watch and listen.

Once you have the hang of this, try it when you are with your partner, a family member or a close friend. Watch and listen without getting lost in labels, in descriptions of what they should or shouldn't do or be. Be curious instead.

Minds love black and white. They love to take a position and to act as if they 'know' what is right and what isn't. This provides a sense of a separate identity and, in that, we become separate from those we love. Knowing how they 'should' be prevents us from appreciating them as they are.

Step out of labelling today and learn to see clearly, and you will start to appreciate that which you hated and to laugh at that which made you angry. You will start to love the person you are with, instead of the one your mind is imagining. And that doesn't mean you have to stay with them, it means that, stay or go, you will enjoy the life that is unfolding around you, no matter how it appears.

Day 3: Helpfulness

In relationships that operate mostly on the level of mind and of thinking, there is a tendency to do things for a *reason,* or so it appears. We act in a certain way because that is how we believe one should act in those circumstances. We help others because it is the right thing to do, according to the mind.

This appears nice on the surface, and many mind-identified people are busy trying to be helpful, trying to be good people. But when this is a logical, analytical, thought-based process, it goes way off-kilter and we miss the mark completely.

This type of helpfulness is not wrong, it is skewed because it arises out of a thought and out of the belief in a separate self. Along with this belief, the idea of time arises as we assess 'my past' to see what sort of person I am and plan 'my future' in order that I can become a better person and be happy – hooray! This way of being helpful is therefore a means to an end for the mind, and others can feel that. It's not about you and what you need, it's about my need to be a certain type of person, according to my mind.

And because this all arises in thought, it is not in sync with what arises now. The mind has a set of rules and prescriptions to follow, and it wants them followed. Lost in mind, you are unaware of what is happening this instant and so that old path is followed whether it is appropriate or not. And often it isn't.

We have all been on the end of this type of 'help', where someone else wasn't listening, wasn't interested, and knew what was best for us. Or worse, they *pretended* to listen, *pretended* to be interested, and then did what they wanted anyway!

On the flip side, we have all done this too. But, actually, there was no one 'doing' it. We acted out the conditioning of our minds, lost in thought, unaware of what was going on, so there is no one to blame and no one to feel guilty. That would be the mind again, crafty old thing!

True helpfulness arises naturally when you see a situation clearly. Someone asks for money, you have some, you give it, you forget about it and keep walking. A child falls, you pick them up and look for their parent, you keep walking. All this time the mind is busy thinking, 'Does he really need the money? What will he spend it on?' Or, 'Should I help her up? She's not my child so I wonder if her mum will get upset if I do?'

And by the time the mind has decided what to do (or not), the situation is gone, as it moves at the speed of life, always flowing, always moving.

And in the ongoing relationships of our lives, a subtle and even more destructive habit can sneak in: the tendency to expect something later on. We have all said or thought, 'After all I've done for you, I can't believe you would . . .' The mind is saying that in the past, I helped you, therefore we now have a contract, and you should do certain things (for eternity, probably) in order to honour the deal you didn't strike (because I didn't tell you there was a catch). This doesn't seem all that helpful.

Look without thinking and you will find yourself acting quite naturally. This action is always appropriate to the situation because it comes out of awareness and it comes now. That doesn't mean it always 'works out', according to the mind, only that it is the best possible response in this instant.

This all becomes quite simple when you stop hanging on to this thing called 'the past'.

Activity – Letting Go of the Past

For one day, try a simple experiment. Act in all your relationships as if you have no past.

Before we go further, I don't mean you should introduce yourself to your partner in the morning and act as if you had never met, rather that you should leave the past out of your interactions.

Drop what they did yesterday, what you did yesterday, and be with them in the space of this moment. Breathe, watch, listen and enjoy.

If help is asked for, give it; otherwise, just stay with your own beautiful presence, now.

If something obviously is needed, if someone falls, if they need some money, if you see they forgot their wallet, then help, if you can, and then forget about it. Once that action is done, drop it.

Don't carry on thinking about how great you are or how ungrateful they were, or anything else. Drop it like a hot potato.

And when you are helping another, leave any idea of future outcomes alone. It's their business whether they like it, whether they use it, whether they enjoy it. Love doing it so much that it doesn't matter what happens next. Drop the future like a hot potato too.

Try this today and see what happens in your life.

When you stop trying to enhance your image of yourself as a helpful person, then there is room to help. But you don't get credit and you can't predict the outcome. Helping is an end in itself, an expression of your wonderful self. Enjoy it for its own sake, and leave the rest alone.

You'll be glad you did, and others will be grateful too!

Day 4: Knowing Your Place

In our minds, there are many characters in this thing called life, many images of other people. And when we get lost in this world, life can become like a soap opera in many ways, with drama, intrigue and excitement permeating our experience.

This is the world of mind and of appearance, where things come and go continuously, and the thinking mind gives a running commentary on what has happened and what it all means. Without that commentary, there would be no things, no people in your experience. You would still see the images, but without words to call them 'things', 'people', 'Oli', 'tree', there would only be the direct experience of seeing.

Within relationships you can observe this happening too. Try looking at your loved one without using words, without using the alphabet. They are still there in your vision now, but the one who usually runs the show (the 'me' show, that is), the one who chatters and tells you what it all means, isn't there without the words. This leaves the experience itself and the one who is watching it unfold, and that is you.

After all, when labelling stops, something remains, someone is still there watching the whole thing, right? That's who you are, or what you are. But you can't see it, you can't describe it and nothing I say about it here will be right, but you can experience it directly.

Up until this point, you have probably simply identified

with the voice that does all the talking and done what it said, the same as the rest of us. You probably felt happy when it said things were good and sad when it said things were bad – again, the same as everybody else.

Instead of experiencing this moment directly, you were drawn into this world of abstraction, in which the past is pulled apart, dissected, analysed and projected into a so-called 'future'. And to this voice, your loved ones were merely objects like everything else, more props in the story of you.

But if you haven't taken this book back or thrown it away yet, then there is a movement happening within you. It is time to move beyond this thought-based reality and experience your life right now. And if you picture attention as a thing that can move between different places, it is moving from the outer world and the thoughts about that world, to the inner world and the experience that arises from it.

The old way was to look outside for happiness, listen to the mental commentary about what was seen and heard out there, then figure out what to do next. This new way is to start within, to stay aware of your self as you move through the world and to experience what arises without thinking about it. And I call this way of relating 'Knowing Your Place'.

Activity – Knowing Your Place

Find a quiet spot to start this activity. Close your eyes, feel the breath and be still.

Notice that there is awareness of each breath, thought and sensation that arises, and direct your attention to that awareness.

Allow your attention to sink into the body, and watch everything come and go.

When you are ready, continue with your day, and see if it is possible to stay in this place, this pure, aware watching, as you relate to your friends and loved ones. As you will see, it is perfectly possible to live skilfully without thinking about and labelling everything that happens, without being lost in that voice. In fact, it's much easier than the 'normal' way of living!

This week, play with the practice of being there as the watcher of all that arises, without getting involved in the mind chatter that desperately wants your attention.

The mind would say that it is impossible to live without thinking about what you will do and what is happening, but this is an error of perception. Watch how you cross the road and you will see how it is wordless, how you don't think about how far away the cars are and how fast they are moving; you look, and when it appears safe, the body moves. You might even manage it while you are thinking about something completely different!

And relationships are no different. When you find the awareness within and relate from there, loving others is natural, being your best is effortless and everything becomes a lot of fun – plenty of laughs and not such a serious undertone, because that arose through thinking.

It's safe to throw that away as your primary place of residence. It's safe to move back to your true home and live from there. Life will take care of the rest by itself.

But start small today, play with this way of living and see what happens, see if the world collapses. You will be pleasantly surprised, I promise you.

Day 5: Beyond Avoidance

Many people, including myself, would describe themselves as conflict avoiders, as people who prefer to maintain harmony on the surface, at almost any cost. For me, this way of living was a way to avoid the uncomfortable feeling that came when there was apparent discord. I felt uncomfortable in such situations and so, in all my relationships, I tried to maintain this superficial harmony until the strain became too great and I would either snap, or run away from the situation.

In some ways I admired those who seemed at ease in conflict, although I thought it strange that some people tried to seek it. And although I still don't actively seek conflict with others, I have learnt, through applying mindfulness to my relationships, that sometimes some turbulence is required to move relationships to a deeper level.

Underneath surface harmony, there is often unspoken tension, which the mind loves. Your mind wants conflict because it wants to resist, and it wants to resist because resistance gives you a stronger sense of identity. It is easier to feel like you're someone when you stand against something (or someone) else, after all! The combination of some underlying tension with the desire to avoid conflict allows the mind to play all day, thinking about the drama, plotting possible actions to deal with it, and even discussing the situation with others.

This is the basic plot for many TV shows too, an underlying surface tension that drags you along but is never completely resolved, and if you see the popularity of shows based on this principle, you will see how much the human mind loves it! In the same way, many people who start to practise mindfulness notice that their lives have moved from one drama to the next, like a soap opera. And, if you aren't careful, your mindfulness practice can become a way to cover up that tension, so you can keep avoiding it.

When I started practising mindfulness in 2003 or 2004 (I can't quite remember when it was!), I was hoping to escape from pain. When I started to experience a deeper sense of peace, it seemed logical that I could avoid conflict even more. If situations are less distressing and emotions are easier to deal with, then there is not much need to talk honestly with people about things you see as problems. It's easier, seemingly, to deal with things internally.

As a starting point, this is not so bad. As discussed in other parts of this book, starting by working through and clarifying what is happening within is a great way to make sure your actions come from a peaceful, contented place. But you may notice, still, that some of the things others do don't sit well with you, and this is where a simple conversation can be the most helpful path forward.

Recently, a colleague was behaving in a way that I thought was out of sync with the way our team works. After noticing that I was in a conflict-avoidant mindset, I decided to talk with them directly instead. I stated clearly what I had noticed and what I felt, then I sat back and listened mindfully, taking in their words with awareness, clarity and alertness. I didn't sit and evaluate their words, I didn't try to make them wrong (and me right), and I allowed them to have their own view of the situation. We came to an understanding, then we were able to move on – simple.

But before I raised this conversation, I spent a week stewing needlessly. And as I look back on that week, I can see the warning signs, which might prevent you from needing to stew, if you can spot them early.

Activity – Beyond Avoidance

Bring to mind a recent (or current) conflict that you downplayed or avoided to some extent. As you do so, you will probably recognise some of the warning signs that I noticed when I looked back on my week of stewing:

- Complaining. I noticed I was complaining in my head, and to other people, about the situation, but not talking to the person involved.
- False powerlessness. I convinced myself that there was nothing I could do until *they* changed. But there was something I could do. I could tell them.
- Avoidance. I avoided that person, didn't ask about the situation and tried to focus on other things, but it kept popping into my mind.

When you notice these (or your own) signs arising, try these steps:

- Take a mindful breath or two. Bring yourself completely into the moment.
- Arrange to speak with the person involved.
- Tell them how you feel and what you noticed.
- Listen and allow them to respond however they do.

Try this today. Don't back out, as you'll only waste energy on stewing. Instead of resorting to complaints and false powerlessness, use a disagreement as an opportunity to deepen your relationship with another. Don't blame or attack, just explain.

For example: 'I noticed that you didn't discuss that process with me. I felt shut out and now I'm noticing that I don't want to work here so much anymore.'

There's no blame, only the description of an experience. Adapt this to your own situation and you will discover that hiding underneath every disagreement is a chance to become closer to another.

Day 6: When They Won't Change

Yesterday, we explored how we can be honest and direct in our relationships, sharing what we feel with those we love. But sometimes the mind wants to share in this with a hidden (or not so hidden) agenda: to make the other person change.

Mindful honesty has no agenda, it is the act of saying what comes naturally, what occurs to you in a particular situation. There is no need for the other person to hear it, understand it, or do anything with it, we just speak.

Often, once we have spoken about how we feel about a particular thing, we hope that others will then adjust their behaviour to better suit our preferences, but what if they don't? What if you tell your partner that you would like him to help out more around the house and he doesn't? What if you tell your friend that you want her to listen more and judge less, but she won't? These experiences are a wonderful gift for several reasons, but it can be difficult to see this at the time.

The power of being surrounded by rigid, seemingly difficult people is that it prevents you from finding comfort and satisfaction in the outside world. These people will not change to suit your preferences. They will not listen to what you have to say, and if they do catch a word or two, there is zero chance that they will act on it. This is nothing personal. It's just that they are captivated by the stories in their heads.

They won't change, so where will you look to find happiness? If it can't be found outside, then you must look in the one place the mind most wants to avoid: within.

The sooner we stop looking to others to provide us with a comfortable, satisfying life, the sooner we can start looking for the truth that hides within. Whenever you feel upset, frustrated, dissatisfied or angry, you will know that you were expecting something that you didn't get! Let's use that partner who doesn't help around the house as an example. You ask and you ask and he still doesn't lift a finger, and your mind starts going mad, complaining, telling stories about what he 'should' be doing and generally arguing with life.

He should help! But he doesn't. He should listen! But he doesn't. So you only have two choices if you want to be sane.

Activity – Making the Choice

When faced with this situation, if you want to be at peace, you need to start with one shift: allowing what is to be what it is. You need to shift attention from the outside (him) to your inner world and allow the anger, frustration and stories to come and go. Once you have made this shift, you have two sane options:

1) Allow the situation to continue and stay in it.

If you want to or have to stay in the situation, you can stay sane by allowing it to be. You can still be assertive, honest and prevent others from harming you, if that's possible, but don't dwell on what happened mentally. Stay with what is here now and let the experience be as it is.

For example, you could accept that your partner isn't helpful and that you have chosen to stay with him. You can then mindfully do the jobs around the house (you might even enjoy them), and you can keep asking him for help too. The difference is that, when you allow what is, there is no anger or frustration when he doesn't come up with the goods!

2) Allow the situation to continue and leave it.

You can also (if possible) accept the situation as it is and leave it without a hint of anger. For example, you might say to your partner: 'I love you but I want to be with someone who helps around the house. Goodbye.' And then you could move on with your life without any animosity or sadness, only joy and empowerment.

Take a moment now to consider a situation you have been arguing with mentally and make a choice. Will you stay and work with the situation, or will you peacefully move on? Spend some time imagining what each option might look like and notice how different it would feel to the usual pattern of resistance and control.

To the mind, allowing seems like a powerless act, but it is quite the opposite. After all, when you are mentally arguing with someone's behaviour, they have all the power, they control your happiness in that moment. Don't you want to take that power back?

With great responsibility comes great power. Take responsibility for your own inner state, always, and you will discover that the power was yours all along. You only thought you could give it away to somebody else.

Day 7: Loving Wholeheartedly

Living lost in thought, it is impossible to live or to love wholeheartedly, because we are always thinking about the future, or daydreaming about something other than this. But it is also possible to use mindfulness practice, or any type of meditation, as a sort of escape, as a way to avoid the full experience of life.

If you become numb and uncaring, then the pain will be lessened, or so the mind believes. You might find at some points on your journey therefore that you are seeking to avoid discomfort by 'living in the now'.

People often tell me that they are experiencing some sadness or anger, and are trying to get back to peace. I call this 'trying to mindfulness it away'. It's the mind at work, analysing what is and saying, 'Do some mindfulness and we should be OK. If you do it properly, of course.'

But if you are trying to escape this moment, that's not mindfulness, it's more of the same old resistance! Mindfulness is the full experience of what is, with no gaps, no filters, no 'yes but'. When you practise mindfulness, the future (which is merely a thought) dissolves, so you can't use it to get to a 'better' future.

When we are lost in mind like this, we become small, petty, focused on our own set of demands. But when you enter this mindful space with your attention, there is room for everything that arises. You can love what *is* wholeheartedly. Perhaps it would be better to say that love just happens in this space, because in true practice there is no one there to do the loving. There is no gap between you as the watcher and what arises.

If the thought 'I am trying to love wholeheartedly' arises, that 'I' is the one that's in the way! For that 'I' thought to arise, there has to be a separation between awareness and what arises. There has to be a time gap in which the mind produces these thoughts, analyses what has been perceived and labels and comments.

How then can we love wholeheartedly, if there is no time to think about it? The key is to be there as awareness, as the witness of what is happening, not as the imagined I, the self-image. As this awareness comes to the front of your experience, and as thinking moves to the back, love flows naturally and nothing will get in its way.

Activity – Awareness in Love

Close your eyes for a moment and breathe. As you do so, imagine that you are not a person with a past and a future, imagine that you are the energy that creates everything in your world, taking this shape, appearing as a person.

As you imagine this, notice the awareness in the background of your experience and imagine that this is how that energy moves in the world, how you move in the world.

And imagine that this awareness loves to be, loves to watch the energy change into all these different shapes, without holding any above any others, so that anger, joy, rain, sun, rabbits and rats are all equal to it.

Open your eyes and sit for a few minutes as if you are that, looking around the world and marvelling at the things you see now.

And when you meet your loved ones today, act as if they are a part of the show too, and love them as expressions of that energy, not as people with a past and a future. Love them right now.

I said 'imagine' a lot there, but it is pretty clear when you look that we are all made up of the same energy and we all are that awareness that watches. And when you see this, not believe it but see it, then loving wholeheartedly is natural.

In fact, the only thing that ever gets in the way of loving like that is the thinking mind, or getting lost in thought, to be more precise. When you go into who you are before and after thoughts have taken over, you will find a natural clarity, peace and stillness. And it is out of that stillness that all this wonderful, unconditional love emerges.

In a way, you can't create it, learn it or even do it. All you can do is to explore that stillness with your attention until it moves by itself. Look, look, look!

Keep looking and all will become clear.

WEEK 6

Separately Together

This week, as we come to the end of our journey together, we will flip all our traditional beliefs and concepts about relationships upside down and have a look at them to see if they are true. All of these beliefs hinge on the understanding that we are two separate people having separate experiences, but as you will see, this is not so easy to verify. If we stick with what you can see, feel and experience directly, the world of relationships is very different from what your mind projects.

What you will learn this week is that you are the only one whose existence you can verify, and while this aloneness may sound scary or silly to the mind, when it is seen as the truth of your experience, it is an incredible relief. Imagine never having to worry about what another is thinking or experiencing, either 'out there' in the so-called world or in your direct experience. This is what you will experience when you begin to see clearly.

'But won't this make me callous, cold and uncaring?' asks the mind. No. On the contrary, seeing that you are the only one whose existence you can be sure of releases you from all fear, and from the need to get anything from others. In this completeness, the love and compassion you feel for what you see, including people, animals and plants, is overpowering. You won't be able to do anything *but* be caring.

This is quite a journey, and your mind may struggle to keep up, so don't feel you have to understand or agree/disagree with what you read. Look upon it like the proposal for an experiment you are about to conduct, without knowing what the outcome will be. This is the most profound, most wonderful experiment the human race is yet to attempt: the search to find out what is real and can be verified, and what is imagined.

Let's begin.

Day 1: Only Me

I recently discovered something astounding. I am the only person I can definitely say exists. Now before you go saying I've gone crazy or turned narcissistic, let me explain what I mean.

As I walk around the world, I see people like you do. But when you see them, your mind tells a story about them, and gives them an identity, and from this identity an image of 'John' or 'Judy' arises. And then you say, 'That's my friend John' or, 'That's Judy, she's horrible' – more stories.

But when thinking stops for a moment and those stories aren't there demanding attention, you can notice that we never actually see people. We see images that look like people (which is another concept based on the past). We touch things that feel like people (according to concepts again). And then there is you, the one being you know is here.

Now I am not saying that nobody else exists, that none of these image people I see are having this experience we call being human. I'm only saying that I can't verify that based on my own experience. I see and hear things, and the mind then assumes that means John and Judy are real, solid, and then assigns them labels. All this arises from and supports our sense of separateness, which you will also see as false.

This all might sound like some strange philosophical paradox, but it is no more or less than what I notice, and you can check it out for yourself (maybe your experience is different). Who can you be certain exists based on your experience, not on assumption? Who can be verified as being? If you look, you will see that you are the protagonist in your own little movie, your own universe that exists for now and will dissolve quite soon.

And the constant projection of others, the focus on what they do, think and feel (according to our imagination) is perhaps the biggest barrier to looking within and discovering your own essence. I know it sounds mad, as it is completely contrary to what we have believed forever, but if you treat yourself as the only one here, you will start to look deeper within, and you will become a blessing to those around you.

Don't believe me, though. Try this little experiment and see what you find out.

Activity – Who is There?

Today, as you interact with the world around you, try a little test. Continue to mentally label what you see and hear, but only as you experience it, not as you believe it to be.

For example, when your partner wakes up in the morning and you see him or her for the first time today, look closely without using memory and see if you can be sure that they exist. You can see an image of a person (even 'person' is a story, but let's leave that for today), your hands touch something we call skin. Is there an identity over there that is different from yours?

What can you be certain of, based on your experience? There is an image, some sounds arising and sensory activity. And where is all this arising? Is it happening 'out there' in 'the world', or is it happening in you, now? Where is sound perceived – in you or out there? Where is the image seen – in you or out there?

Check all of this thoroughly and don't let your mind take a shortcut. The truth will surprise you!

In the relationships in my apparent life, all I see are images of what I call people, coming and going. All of it happens within this oval-shaped window that is my universe, and I trust that what comes into that oval is what needs my attention.

Yesterday I was at the park with a group my wife organises. There were some people I knew and some I didn't, and 15 or 20 children from a number of families. Walking through the park, I saw images, some kids playing, some kids not playing. Some kids looking comfortable, some kids looking nervous. Naturally my attention was drawn to those who looked nervous, and where the attention goes, the body follows.

I found this body and mind organising a game that all those kids took part in, not because I thought I should, not because I felt bad, not for any reason, because it arose from beyond thought. It was life looking after life, if you will, as I see no difference between that child and my child, between my child and me. There is no separate person here to make that distinction.

And this is the reality of living in the simplicity of just this, just now. Live your *experience*, not your imagination, and you will know that you are the only one who is here watching. In this realisation, there is nothing left but compassion, love and joy.

All this might make your mind spin! But keep it simple, look into your experience and ask yourself: 'What can I be sure of right now?' Sit with that question and see what arises.

Day 2: True Love

What we usually call love is confusing and confused, a misperception of reality that keeps us at the mercy of the world around us and the people who appear within that world. This love is located somewhere 'out there', and is dependent on some other person. That person also needs to keep doing certain things and not doing other things, otherwise the heart gets broken.

And as well as romantic relationships, this same principle applies to friendships, family relationships and others. When the people we relate to meet the criteria of the mind, we feel loved, and when they don't, we feel unloved.

We talk as if love were like sunlight, something that radiates from a body out there and either shines on me or doesn't, depending on the season and the conditions. Where is this love that is dependent on other people and what is it made of? Hold this idea, that others generate that feeling of being loved, up to the light of awareness and you will see it was never so. It was all in you.

When you are sitting alone at night and you feel loved as you remember all the nice things that happened today, who is that feeling arising in and from? Are your friends and family still madly sending you telepathic love rays? Or is it arising in and from you?

And when you sit alone and disheartened, feeling unloved and as if no one cares, who is generating that feeling? There's no one else there, so that only leaves you!

The mind replays certain mental movies that fit the story you are enthralled in at this point in your life. If your story is about how great life is, your mind replays the lovely things people did or said and your body responds to those stories. Or if the story is a sad one, a different movie plays and you feel cold and lonely.

It's like being at the cinema. Images flash across the screen and your body responds with laughter, or tears, or smiles, but only if you are fully engaged in the story and the images, only if you connect with them. If you sit talking to the person next to you or texting on your phone, the story won't have the same impact. The emotional reaction is reliant on your attention, and on your identification with the characters, and the mental movies are the same.

Having recognised this, it might be tempting (for the mind, anyway) to try to project more positive movies so that you feel good more of the time, but this is unnecessary and counterproductive if you want to find true love.

True love has two forms. The first is the love of being, the joy of being what you are, without needing anything added to it. This love is completely self-sufficient, and is not dependent on any outside conditions. The second is when this same love is expressed, when it moves into the world around you. When this happens, your kindness and compassion are naturally expressed, regardless of what is going on out in the world.

Whatever form this love takes, though, it has nothing to do with thinking, with stories, or with time. It is you experiencing yourself without all that mental chatter getting in the way. Sometimes this feeling is dormant, and sometimes it flows out, all by itself.

If you have lived under the spell of negative stories about yourself for a long time, the idea that love is your natural state, and that it doesn't depend on anything outside of you, may seem a bit hard to believe. And you shouldn't believe it, as only your mind can do that. Instead, go inside and see what is true for you.

Activity – True Love

Close your eyes for a moment and feel yourself breathing. Follow the in-breath with your attention, then smile and let your shoulders relax as you breathe out.

As you breathe and smile, take your attention into the body and notice all the different sensations you can feel. Don't label anything, just feel everything. Let your whole body relax into this moment with every out-breath.

Now, without thinking about what was or what will be, allow your attention to rest in this space, this now, and keep smiling. Notice how wonderful it is to breathe, to be. Enjoy that.

Whatever thoughts and emotions are there, let them be. This is the experience of yourself, and those thoughts and feelings don't need to leave or change for you to be yourself. Leave the thoughts alone. Feel the emotions without labelling them. Just be.

Stay with this practice for as long as you like, and come back to it often. As you get more familiar with yourself, this awareness will naturally start to express itself in the world around you.

True love is not a belief or a story, and it depends on no one else. It is the simple joy of being, and when you realise this experientially, you will see that no one ever needs to do anything in particular for you to feel loved. You are love, so how could you be separate from it? And as all that mind stuff is recognised for what it is, it will drop, and you will naturally become an expression of this love in the world.

Day 3: When You're Alone

Most humans carry their friends, family and loved ones around with them all day long. You can see this in their need (and yours) to talk about others, think about others and recreate stories of the past, of what they did or didn't do. This is such a normal, natural thing for most people that we don't even notice that it *is* a thing. We're so caught up in those mind stories of others that we confuse the stories for the actual people, and we don't realise that we're imagining the whole thing.

My friend May is a great example of this. Whenever we meet, she tells stories of the people in her life, stories that are mostly loving and funny, sometimes upset or angry, and as she speaks, I can see that those people are here with us at that moment. To be more accurate, a trace of their reflection is here, like an echo bouncing up and down in a cave. And as May tells the stories of those people, I can see her view of them changing, her opinion shifting during the conversation. In this way, our stories create the image of who that person is to us, but it is only an image.

After all, as May and I chat, the only ones in the room are her and me. The people she describes could just as well be from a TV show or a book she is reading. But the mind is hypnotised by its creation, and it believes that when the thought, the image of that person arises, it is accurate, true and that it represents the people themselves.

This is why we can get into an argument with another person without them being there physically. The mind does the whole thing. It is also why we can laugh at the antics of someone who is miles away and why we worry about the fortunes of people who are nowhere near us. The mind sees the image and the person as connected, as one almost, and this is the root of much trouble.

Carrying all your loved ones (as well as those you don't much like) around in your head is a tiring business, as like a bus full of school children, there is always at least one calling for your attention. And when things appear to 'go wrong' in relationships, these people in your head will torture and torment you, absorbing almost all of your attention and energy, and creating stress and worry.

When you feel stressed about a situation, you can notice this by considering how long the event lasted and comparing that with how long you spent lost in thoughts *about* the situation. Mostly the events, behaviours and words we get upset about last only a few seconds, but the stories can continue for the rest of your life if you keep feeding them. Some even manage to keep the story alive after they have forgotten the initial event, staying angry with someone for decades over something they can't remember.

When I realised this tendency in myself, to continually think about people who aren't here, I looked into it deeply, to see if it had any purpose, if there was a reason to keep doing it. What I found was not a reason, but an addiction to thinking and storytelling. I discovered that something in me loved that retelling of the past, and that something is my thinking mind.

The thinking mind keeps itself alive by capturing your attention, drawing you into these stories and using the energy you provide to keep building on them. Without your attention, the stories fade quickly and there is more and more silence. The thinking mind is not a fan of silence, so there is an urge to keep thinking, analysing and wondering, but all this can be dropped quite easily with a little practice.

Activity – Only You

Today I invite you to run a mental experiment to see what it is like to leave others alone unless they need your attention. Try this for a day and see what happens.

When you are with someone else, or talking on the phone or emailing even, give them your total attention (unless you have small children, then just do your best). Look and listen mindfully and take in all that they have to say.

Once that interaction ends, leave it alone unless there is some practical thing you need to do (such as write something on the calendar, make an appointment, etc.). Be alone, and turn your attention inward. Feel your breath and body and be curious about your inner experience now.

When the mind starts to retell the stories of others, leave them alone. Stay with your experience of you, now, or of what you are doing now.

For today, make a choice not to spend your attention on anyone else unless they are here or unless it is necessary to do so for a practical reason. Be totally with whoever is here now, and if that is only you, then pay this attention to you and see what happens.

In fact, we are not paying less attention to the person, we are withdrawing our attention from the story, which has nothing to do with them. While the mind may say that this will make you cold and aloof, the opposite is true. It frees you to turn inward and to be present with the person here now, instead of that imagined person in your mind.

And in this, there is freedom, peace and love, and all around you will feel that.

Day 4: Speaking to Myself

Perhaps the most sacred belief of the mind is that I exist as something separate from everyone and everything else around me. There is a sense of separation that arises in childhood and grows stronger over the years, until we have an image of ourselves as completely apart from the world and everyone else. I and others.

I like to call this 'self-image', because it is a sort of mental picture made up of words, memories and images. When I had a strong sense of self, for example, I thought of myself as 'funny'; this was part of my self-image. And what was this concept made of? It was made of memory, of remembered images of me saying something and others laughing – pretty fragile stuff. And due to this fragility, I had to keep trying to make others laugh in order to maintain that part of 'me'.

I remember travelling in the Americas for a few months and being unable to make anyone laugh, as the sense of humour there was quite different from that in Australia. I felt quite depressed that I had 'lost' a part of 'me'. Isn't that funny? My mind created a concept based on memory (which is a reflection of something that doesn't exist), and when that concept couldn't be sustained, sadness arose. That's how strong the mind is!

This self-image is what everyone is referring to when they say, 'I like . . .' and, 'I wish I could . . .' It's their imaginary friend! And what the mind does in relationships is to continuously tell the story of how this self-image is relating to the others that it seems to interact with. It analyses the responses of others to the image that is put forward and then comments, 'She loves me, she loves me not . . .' and so on.

When most people are talking to someone else, they feel a sense of separateness from that person, because their self-image is largely built on comparison and on how they are better or worse than someone else.

But look closely at your actual experience (as opposed to what your mind says) and you will notice a few differences that contradict these sacred beliefs. Firstly, if you look deep inside yourself, close your eyes and take attention into your body, you will find that no one is home. There are thoughts, feelings and sensations arising in you and dissolving, but this 'me' can't be located. All those phenomena arise in space and disappear in space, that's all. When they disappear, you're still here, so you must be the space. This isn't a belief or an affirmation, it's what I have found when I finally bothered to look. Close your eyes now and see if this is true for you.

Underneath all their conditioning, others are like this too: empty space in which stuff is arising. In this, we are the same. All that seems different, if you examine it, is actually made of concepts, beliefs that have been layered on top of us since we started to understand language. As those beliefs dissolve, you will see, not believe, that everyone is the same thing (or the same no-thing) in a different costume.

And while I know many people make these sorts of statements in new-age discourse, they are more often describing what they believe, not what they see. What I am pointing to is my actual experience.

In relationships, everyone is the same! We still play the role of 'John' and 'Suzie', but what we are underneath these outfits is identical. And when you recognise this in your own experience, the self-image and the sense of separation start to drop all at the same time. What's left feels like me interacting with me, purely for the fun of it, with no one to enhance or protect from 'you'. It's very freeing.

You can start to explore this with an activity that invites you to examine more closely the details of your experience now.

Activity – Who's Talking?

Try this the next time you are talking with another person. See if you can stay present and listen to what they're saying without dissecting and analysing their words. Allow the words to come and go.

Notice how the words arise and disappear in you, in the awareness that you are, and notice how, when you speak, the same thing happens. Words come and go, but this time from your mouth.

You may be aware that those words come by themselves, and often you don't know what will be said until it comes out, just like when the other person is talking.

On both ends of the conversation, words are arising out of nowhere, and disappearing again, witnessed by two examples of that awareness in costume.

Look deeply into your conversations this week and see if this is so.

Don't believe a word of what you read today, test it out for yourself instead. See what you find when you look into yourself, and notice what happens in conversation when you are alert and present.

Keep looking, don't listen to the mind, and you will make some incredible discoveries.

Day 5: Where Conflict Happens

For most human beings, conflict is a part of their daily reality in some form. Conflict out there and conflict in here, or so it seems at least. We run into difficulty when those around us want different things or have different beliefs, and we experience conflict with the world around us when we mentally argue, complain and criticise.

And to those completely lost in mind, it always appears that conflict is caused by some event 'out there'. It looks as if someone did something wrong, and that caused the problem, but as we have discovered already, our internal response to what is has a far greater influence on what we experience than the actions of others.

Today we will explore the primary conflict, the inner disagreement with reality, from which all other conflicts stem. The only way to resolve our troubles as a species and as individuals is to resolve this conflict first, and then see what we can do in the outside world, rather than the other way around.

As a starting point, let's explore an example of a typical relationship event and dig a little deeper into the nature of the conflict that it appears to generate. Imagine for a moment that your partner of many years leaves you unexpectedly (for you, anyway) and moves in with someone else. This is considered just about the ultimate betrayal by the mind (and I'm not saying it's a good idea either), and to most it will appear as if he is the *cause* of the conflict. His behaviour made me feel sad, angry, upset and so on.

But let's look a little deeper, because, in spite of the amazing variability out in the world, the infinite variety of things that can happen, conflict is always the same at its source. It begins from a simple combination: there is a strong sense of 'me' (the self-image we looked at earlier), which has a belief in what should happen and then something else happens instead.

In this case, there is a belief that he should have stayed, that he was wrong to leave and that you will never find someone else. The mind had projected a future together and the loss of that leaves a hole in the sense of identity, as does the absence of the partner you saw as part of your world.

Underneath all of this, there is a bundle of thoughts that know better than life and enter into a conflict with what is.

Now, if the person is imagined, as I say (which, of course, you should verify for yourself), is no more real than the monster can be under your child's bed. The *belief* in that person is enough to cause all the trouble, just as the belief in a monster prevents a child from sleeping. It's the same principle. Without the belief in the self-image and it's imagined future, no suffering is possible.

Of course, I am not saying that you don't exist. You are there reading these words, I know. The imagined part is all the concepts you layer on top of yourself, the identity you believe in that is made up of memory and belief.

Also, there is no problem with any emotion that arises in this type of situation. If you feel sad, angry, upset, lost or whatever, it's fine, because you can *use* these emotions to point you back to the clarity and simplicity of mindfulness. Your mind (the one who created the stories that gave rise to the emotions) will tell you that you're failing at mindfulness because you are suffering, but leave that story alone and look into your experience instead. The following activity will show you how to get started.

Activity – Who?

When things like this happen in your world, if you can, don't get drawn into an argument with any of it, not with the event and not with what you feel when you remember it.

Instead, close your eyes, go deep within and ask yourself these questions, and be sure to sit still and let the answers come on their own, if they do:

- Who is upset right now?
- Is there someone who is hurt, or only a feeling I call 'hurt' arising?
- What is that feeling arising in? Is it in 'me', or is it arising in space?
- Is there someone here who owns that feeling?
- If the feeling arises and falls in space, and the space remains, which one is me?

There is no need to answer these questions in words, they are pointers to direct your attention within. Try them over the next few days with minor upsets and conflicts with what is. You won't regret it.

There is no need to end inner conflict through effort or willpower, that's merely resistance in disguise. Instead, make conflict your friend, and use it to go deeper inside, to know yourself more fully, and to put an end to your troubles, once and for all.

Day 6: Connected to Everyone

These days, as people keep telling me, many humans are becoming increasingly disconnected from each other. In the last few hundred years, in the Western world at least, the social systems that kept us close as people have all been rapidly dissolving. And with the rise of the internet and social media, this dissolution has increased in speed as we spend more time relating to friends virtually and less time face to face or on the phone.

All this can make it appear as if something went wrong, as if we 'should' be connected as we were in the 'good old days', but the universe doesn't make mistakes, in my experience. What is dissolving is not connectedness as such, but our sense of collective identity, which also gave rise to the 'us' that was fearful of 'them', be they the villagers over the hill or the people over the other side of the world. This is all dissolving before our eyes.

This can leave people feeling a little lost and disconnected, because the mind tends to associate 'connection' with certain people, whom you need to see regularly in order to feel OK about the world. It labels some as 'friends', which then leaves the rest as 'not friends' or 'strangers', and if those friends are too busy or too far away, or if the friendship breaks down, there is a feeling of loneliness that can creep in.

The mechanics of this are quite simple: you are with someone (be that yourself or someone else) and your mind says you should be with someone else. We have seen this before, haven't we? It's the basic operation of the mind in another form: see what is, compare it with what isn't, tell stories about why it's wrong.

In reality, if you are deeply in touch with who you are underneath all this mind stuff, there is no possibility of loneliness. And when you venture out into the world mindfully, you are always surrounded by friends. Today you will discover the source of connection – your inner self – and you will see what a wonderful opportunity it can be to spend time alone. Let's begin.

In a sense, there are two types of connections: those formed by minds talking, discussing and perhaps even agreeing with each other – I'll call these 'mind connections' – and connections that are formed beyond words, thinking and discussion – which I will call 'mindful connections'. The first kind is most common, and most fragile, because this type of connection can only be sustained if we 'like' each other, if we're in general agreement.

Mindful connections arise from the you that is there before words arise and after they fall, the you that was there before you learnt your name and your place in the world – your true self. I am calling it your 'true self' because everything else (concepts, ideas, beliefs) was layered *on top of* that self, like many sets of clothes. Underneath it all, you remain, but it's hard to see you through all those outfits.

The basis of mindful connections is first rediscovering who you are before thought and belief is added, and this is what today's activity points to.

Activity – Underneath

Close your eyes for a moment and feel yourself breathing. You are about to go inside and look for yourself, using a simple question, but first establish your attention in the now, follow your breath and leave thoughts alone.

Next, introduce this question, but please don't try to answer it! The answer can be seen and felt but not thought, so the mind can take a break for a minute. Ask yourself the question, notice the breath, and look into yourself to see what is there. Here is the question:

Who was I before I started thinking?

There was a time when thought had not yet begun because language made no sense to you yet. You had no idea who you were, you just lived, you just were! Who were you then?

As you look with your attention, you will find a sort of empty inner space that is alive and vibrant. Stay with the awareness of that. Connect with yourself.

If your mind got in the way and you didn't find this space within, don't worry. Keep coming back and looking. It is there! And when you discover this space within yourself, then you can return your attention to it whenever you are alone. You can get reacquainted with yourself.

And coming from that place of peace and openness, you will notice a shift in your relationships with others. As my mind has continued to drop away and this awareness has come to the fore, I notice that I never miss 'old friends', although I love to see them when I do. I find that whoever life brings into my world is fine, and I can happily spend as much time with them as the world asks. I don't wish for someone else, or hope for it to end, because only when the mind is in charge can such ideas make any sense.

Because when you see into what is there inside you, you know that everyone else is exactly the same. What could be simpler?

So keep looking, observing, and you too will find yourself in a world full of friends, even when there's no one else there.

Day 7: Your Deepest Loves

As we come to the end of this week, the time has come to look into the relationships that seem to cause the most trouble, and that can bring you to freedom the fastest: the relationships I call your deepest loves. These might be intimate relationships, or the connection with a best friend or your father or your child. In fact, there might be several of these relationships in your life. But before we start, pick one. Pick the relationship that seems to cause you the most difficulty at the moment and focus on it today. Later, you may wish to pick another and re-read these words. Let's get started.

It is not surprising in our thought-identified world that, seemingly, the closer the relationship, the more trouble arises. As relationships deepen, the mind-made self invests more into the idea of a future that includes that person, and as the mind sees the future as the place where happiness will arise, that is a significant investment.

But what if these relationships were seen without thinking, without memory or anticipation? What would you see then?

You would see that either you are with someone now, or they are not a part of your world. You would see that they are the same as you, but wrapped in different conditioning. And you would find yourself simply enjoying this instant together, without projecting into the future, apart from making the plans we all make to help us get along in this world.

To the mind, this sounds silly, or scary, because it removes the whole idea of salvation sometime later, of finding something you don't have now in the future. But there is nothing you can add to yourself later, there is nothing of value that will come to you in the future that isn't here right now. And nothing of value can be given to you by someone else.

This turns the whole game upside down. We have always believed that happiness (which is what everyone is seeking) would come to us in the future through something we don't have now being added, given to us by someone else or by some event. Or the short version: happiness will come (later) from outside me.

What I am saying is the opposite: happiness is here now if you stop chasing it in the future and looking for it outside yourself. Don't expect it from anyone. Don't wait for it. *Look for it now! Look for yourself now!*

This is such a relief. When it dawns on you that you don't need to wait and that no one and nothing can keep you from finding this within yourself, it is incredibly freeing.

Now there are two games. There is the one that matters, the search within, to which you will find yourself devoting more and more energy, and the other, the play without, which pretty much takes care of itself if you leave it alone!

And while the mind may say that you will become uncaring, aloof and distant, quite the opposite is true. Because, once you know that there is nothing you need from the outside world, there is no fear and no greed. Seeing that what you are chasing is inside you, there is no need to manipulate the world to get a certain result. You can just watch and play.

For me, this becomes like playing sport when there is no scoreboard, playing with friends for the fun of playing. No one cares about the outcome, and so people become creative, joyful and caring. If someone falls, you pick them up, and if someone scores, you cheer, regardless of what 'team' they are on.

Activity – Act As If

There's a simple experiment you can do to test out this way of relating to your deepest loves. It is simple, free and powerful, and all you have to do is to *act as if*.

For one day, act as if:

- You don't need anything from them.
- Everything of value is in you already.
- Their presence in your life is an added bonus to what is already perfectly full.

Act as if everything you are seeking is within, and enjoy the play of the world for what it is. Try it today and see what happens when attention moves from the outer to the inner.

The mind may ask, 'How can I act as if this is true?' The answer is simple: take the attention and energy you spent on trying to figure out what your deepest loves were thinking, believing and planning, and look into your own self.

This is the natural movement when it is seen that nothing 'out there' can ever give you what you are looking for.

See through the outer search, drop it completely, and then the real adventure begins!

Conclusion

Welcome to the end of the road. I hope you enjoyed the trip. Since we began this exploration together, we have examined deeply ingrained beliefs, flipped many concepts upside down and hopefully left a lot of heavy baggage along the way. What a journey it has been!

You may have started out looking for a way to 'fix' the relationships in your life, or trying to improve your own way of being with others. As we travelled, I hope that you saw that in fact relationships are a form of mindfulness practice, probably the best form for transforming you. And I hope that you discovered how utterly perfect you are already, whatever your mind may say.

In fact, there is no need to change anything about yourself or anyone else in order to be happy. Happiness will not come in the future through some improvement, it is the lived experience of who you are.

And so, my deepest hope for you, me and humanity as a whole is that we may learn to use thought for practical purposes and otherwise to leave it alone. Believing thoughts has caused so much harm in this world, and I would like to suggest that it's time we moved on.

Of course, that is what is happening, that is why this book exists and why you bothered to read it, because it is time to move beyond thinking as our primary way of being in this world. It is time to wake up and realise that those words and pictures that come and go don't represent us, aren't us, and that we are indeed the awareness that watches the whole show.

So thank you, from the bottom of my heart, for coming on this journey with me. I am always delighted to hear from fellow travellers. Please email oli@peacethroughmindfulness.com.au if you have any questions or just want to say hi.

At the time of writing, there is also a closed Facebook group – called 'Mindfulness with Oli Doyle' – for friends who want support along the way, and who want to support others.

I also have a podcast on iTunes, free apps for iPhone and Android with hundreds of classes in them, and four other mindfulness books if you need more inspiration.

And last of all, I want to encourage you, to plead with you, please, please, please grab hold of the opportunity you have in this life. Turn off the TV, leave your phone in a drawer, and start devoting your spare time to looking into your own self. This is the true journey, and it is rewarding beyond what you could imagine.

Go within, put your energy into seeing clearly the nature of things, and you will be grateful that you did.